ODYSSEY

My Walk to Christ

by

Dr. Leroy V. Swift

JADE Publishing

Darrylyn Z. Swift, Publisher

Point Richmond, California, USA

For information please write to:

JADE Publishing

Darrylyn Z. Swift, Publisher
Point Richmond, California, USA

Discounts on bulk quantities of this publication are available to corporations, educational disciplines, professional associations, and other qualified organizations. For details and specific discount information, and information about the author please contact address above.

Printed in the United States of America:

Leroy V. Swift

An Open Letter

During the past several years I have been thinking about jotting down a few of my thoughts, sharing experiences in my life that would provide you with some ideas of "who" and "what" I am, both now as I write this letter, as well as what I have been and what I have done in my younger years. I wanted you to know also that Jehovah God has blessed me mightily throughout my lifetime and He will bless each of you too if you choose to walk in obedience before Him. Some of you may not have been taught or do not believe in an Almighty God like Jehovah, because you have not been raised to believe in such. For you, I feel a special sadness and hope that through the words I write, you may open your eyes to the truth of God's Word.

There is so much that I would like to share with you, my dears, but I really don't like writing long letters. (I don't even like singing long songs, but that, my dear children, is another story!) However, I have some "*hopes*" for each of you. The main hope that I have, beside you serving God, is that each of you set your sights high and always give life all that you have and Jehovah God will see that you are blessed. The overall purpose of this letter is primarily for the descendants of me, Leroy Victor Swift, and my first wife, Pearl Dietrich Bedford Swift, who is the mother of all of my children, to know me. I also hope that you will one day share it with your off springs so both you and they can gain a better understanding of who your children affectionately call **"Granny Papa"**. I have many grandchildren, so many that I have lost count of them after they numbered more than thirty. I resolved early to never try to keep up with the number of my great grandchildren, nonetheless, from time to time I do like to estimate. I want each of them to know the life I've lived as it too may provide insight to who they are and give them encouragement that they can live in their walk toward Christ, no matter what their past has involved.

I am the father of many children, both natural and spiritual. I have, and have had, many relationships with other people (children) that I love dearly. I hope you too will appreciate the memories that I share in this letter. However, in this letter I will not "name names" nor acknowledge my relationships. Instead, this is my attempt to serve as a "linchpin" between those of my forefathers who came before me and those who will come after me. I want to share some of the unknown facts and stories and some of the, how shall I say this, "idiosyncrasies" of your ancestors. You may even discover some answers to why you are the way you are. Who knows, it may be a characteristic transmitted down through the ages via your ancestor's bloodlines. Another purpose for writing this letter to my offspring is to serve as a painter of "word-pictures" to provide you with a glimpse into how not only my ancestors lived, but even how me and my sisters and brothers lived back in the 1940s and 50s. I know that you cannot imagine what it was like to grow up working in the farm fields harvesting crops while you are dreaming of a better life. I want each of you to know that you have "choices" to make that will determine what kind of life you will have as an adult, and THAT IS ALL LEFT UP TO YOU! You can work hard and apply yourself diligently to getting the best education and the best preparation that you can get, or you can sit around and complain to the world that life is unfair, and that you did not get a fair chance. [NOTE: Whoever told you that life was "fair"? I certainly cannot find that concept in my Bible and I certainly did not experience it in my life]. So, yes, I wanted to paint some word pictures that will open my children's eyes to how life really was and is and how you can overcome.

Finally I am going to provide my children some bits and pieces of my life that they have not been exposed to. I have included several of my sermons, lecture notes and a commentary or two on some contemporary spiritual issues that I feel strongly about. I do hope to also dwell at some point, briefly, about the beginning of the Pearl and Leroy Swift family because, as the mother of all of my offspring, and a woman that I loved beyond measure, she was and still remains the love of my life!

I conceded to write this overview of my life with one provision. As a Christian, as a man of the cloth, in whatever I write I want to share and highlight what I consider to be the crowning achievement in my life. That is MY ACCEPTANCE OF JESUS CHRIST AS MY LORD AND SAVIOUR! I also want to share with you some of my teachings as a Minister, Pastor, Seminary Professor and Evangelist.

So let me tell you a little bit about your family's history and what I call my "Odyssey." You can look that word up if you wish, I imagine that you will find its meaning somewhere in the words to follow. In fact, let's start out with it . . . so here you go!

My niece Freda & children, Cheryl, Matthew, me, Renee,
Darrylyn, sitting on floor

My son Joe and me at his Police Academy Graduation

Me and just a few of my great grandchildren,
all whom I love dearly

Foreword

Before my father shares his Odyssey, I'd like to share mine. It's not my Walk to Christ, I am still working toward that. It is my walk toward understanding. I wrote these words many years ago, and as I was cleaning out some old files, I ran across it. I think it is most fitting to show you my level of understanding of family life as a child, both before and as I grew into a level of maturity. I will not share the entire writing with you, only relevant excerpts.

Let me 'splain it to ya, so's ya understand. I am the descendant of Leroy and Pearl Swift. I was born June 29, 1960 in Kansas City, Missouri after my dad went to find out where my mom had moved while he was away serving his country. Seemed she wanted to be independent and thought a move was in order. How she ever picked Kansas City, I'll never know. But for a young fellow in love, it didn't make a difference where she was, as long as he could be there too. My parents married on June 20, 1958 at St. Stephen's Baptist Church in Kansas City, with Uncle Buster and Aunt Wanda witnessing the proceedings. Uncle Buster and Aunt Wanda aren't on the family tree . . . but I'm here to tell you, their roots are so deeply implanted in me that there is no one in the world that can tell me you have to be from the same blood line for it to count. They, along with my sister Renee, are forever my family. I grew up under them as such, and that's the way it will be when I am no longer on this earth. That's where we were taught to love. My mother loved her brother, Uncle Buster , so much that I was named for him. He is Matthew Bennett. My father loved him such that he allowed her to do it. And my Aunt Wanda - if you don't know her yet, when you meet her you will never forget her.

When my sisters and I were growing up, we thought we were poor. We didn't lack food, clothing, a happy home, nothing. But we thought we were poor. We thought we had to have the best of everything to be considered rich, and we wanted to be rich. I remember we kept being told were rich in love and stuff like that. Hell, I wanted the money! I thought it was normal to travel every year to Houston, sometimes as many as three times a year. And have a camper to go to the lakes with our camping group. And being taken out of school one day so that I could be taken for a helicopter ride with the "nice policeman". That was normal, wasn't it? And the swimming lessons in the summer, where on the ride home dad would let us "guide" him home. And if you didn't tell him to turn the wheel at the right time, there he went, right over the curb! As a matter of fact, I learned to drive by watching EVERYTHING he did behind the wheel.

I even remember thinking my dad didn't really love me. He never showed it. He never said it. He never does anything with me. He mustn't right? I thought that until I was around twenty seven or twenty eight years old. I was in my apartment in California, my girlfriend was pregnant, and I was out of work. In other words, I had plenty of time on my hands. There were a lot of things I couldn't do, besides think. I started remembering the camping trips, the driving sessions, including one when we went camping, just the two of us. When it came time to leave it was always my job to hook up the trailer, which I delighted in doing, since it was the only time I could drive, being only fourteen years old. When I finished, dad would always double check everything and he got in the passenger seat. I didn't say anything to him, just jumped in the driver's seat so I could drive that thing up to the end of the campsite. Boy was I blessed on that day! When we got to the end of the campsite, I stopped at the stop sign, and just before I could put it in park, he said, "You're clear over here." To the highway, I thought. Then I'll give it to him. Seventy miles later, I pulled up in front of our house with the biggest grin that you could have imagined. And you know, for a Swift, that's big!

Then there is the time he woke me up at two in the morning to help him drive his police car across town. And we raced! Again, at fourteen. He taught me how to back the trucks up. Driving was always important to me, even when I was little. He knew that and was giving me what made me happy, no matter what the cost to him. Was I blind, or what? And when that gas stove blew up in my face, you should have seen HIS!. Yep, blind! As a kid I was always interested in cars and trucks. They tried to get me into basketball. I couldn't get that big ole ball into that way too small hole. That's my version anyway. Afterward I would go play with my cars and trucks. Then it was football. At one point someone gave me the ball. When I got up and dusted myself off, I went home and played with my cars and trucks. Then baseball, America's favorite pastime. My dad pitched the ball to his, at that time only son. I finally hit the ball and it went straight to his . . . well, we did get Joe, though. And dad didn't mind me not wanting to play anymore either. Go figure! I went back and started playing with my cars and trucks. As an adult I have been driving a truck that hauls cars since the early 80s. That's right, I'm still playing.

And mom – understanding, supportive, caring, loving - and to think that I didn't like this woman at one point in my life. I wanted so desperately to be away from her. She didn't understand me for any reason. Well, I got my wish. I was sent to Texas to live by my father because that's what I wanted to do. I didn't care about school or anything. All I wanted to do was be away from her – lasted two months! I remember my mother crying with us, over us, for us.

We as kids sometimes forget what our parents are going through just to raise us to be responsible, caring, producing adults. I know now how much my mom and dad have ALWAYS loved me. I just had to grow within to appreciate the rich, full childhood that I was blessed with. And to them I am forever grateful!

Matthew Swift

1

MY WALK BEGINS

I am not sure of the precise moment that I began this long and adventurous journey, this odyssey that I refer to as my *"Walk to Christ"* that I continue to travel now in my 75th year of life. I may answer by saying that it began when I was born in August of 1936 in a small sharecropper's cabin above the rich black "bottom" lands through which the "Little River" continues to flow today, near Gause, Texas, in Milam County. The cabin was not a stunning beauty located in the high altitudes of a mountainous region with exquisite dining or entertainment. No, it was far more. For my family it was home. I remember the two room old wooden structure with well worn siding and a roof that had seen the limitation of its years. Many graced the threshold of our doors and the dusty wooden floors seemed to weaken with each step that was welcomed in. The chinking that prevented the damp air, insects and cold from filtering into the home smelled of sand, mud and forest moss. This was my home, a place of comfort and refuge.

But my life began long before that moment. In my blood flows the mighty blood of unknown African tribes and I dream of unfamiliar thoughts of African celebrations when I was a boy, my mother celebrated for giving birth to a male child who would someday lead his family, and my father honored for raising a warrior, a king who would someday become a man. I dream of a village celebrating my ripened life and I hear the beat of the drums and a lion's roar as the village chief welcomes me into the fold of men. But this dream does not belong to me. I am transported to dreams of which I know to be a parallel reality, a root that is steeped in proverbial truth, it is the family which I know. I close my eyes and imagine the sweltering rays that penetrated the darkened hues of my ancestors. The strength in their faces bears no smiles, but I envision there is love in their eyes. Their heartfelt expressions are masked behind the deep layers of struggle, wisdom and strength that travel across their faces. These Choctaw Indian tribes, who are my ancestors, migrated from the ancient Mexican Empire to the eastern shores of the mighty Mississippi River once dominating what we now call the Mississippi Delta, and the mighty Cherokee tribes who came from the area of Georgia, the Carolinas, and Eastern Tennessee. This is the family I know, standing tall and stoic in their pride, it is this rich texture of my family heritage that I remember well.

On my maternal grandmother's side many of my family are light skinned people, "Mulattos". According to the oral history, our family's lineage is traced back to the Daniel Boone family. A slave girl bore a child to whom I, from a time long before, belong. Although I am called a black man here in these lands I have often thought that, given a choice, I would just refer to myself as a "mongrel", exemplifying the marvelous mixing of the many colors of my forefathers. A tapestry dominated by the dark hues of my African forefathers, coupled with the lighter hues of Indian ancestors.

My grandparents and their children. My mother, Juanita Long
Swift, is in white in the center.

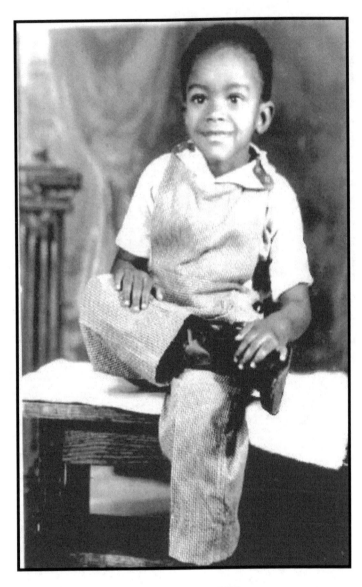

Me as a young child

2

EARLY CHILDHOOD YEARS

I grew up in a little backwoods rural community in Central Texas called Gause. This was a small rural hamlet with a few hundred people whose past and present connected them as family. My family lived about two to three miles out from the township in a black farming settlement called "Two Mile Community". Because my grandfather, August "Gus" Long, owned around six hundred and sixty acres of farm land in Milam County near Gause, and raised cotton, corn, peanuts, sugar cane and water melons, they were considered to be a well-to-do black family. To add to my grandfather's stock, we also kept a large herd of one hundred or so cows and had plenty of hogs, chickens, ducks and other farm animals.

My father, Leroy Swift Sr., had been a sharecropper on the one thousand acre Smith Farm, located in the black land of the Little River Bottoms. It was there that I was born in 1936, in my parent's sharecropper cabin. By the time I could clearly remember, my father and mother had moved over to my grandfather's farm. I enjoyed when my mother would take me back to the place where I was born.

Although I knew this was originally the land on which my family slaved, and I would often recall the stories of the blood, sweat, tears and brutal beatings my ancestors endured, I would always feel a sense of peace and belonging. These feelings contradicted the painful visualization of the stories told and the joys of the family bonds that were created on that very site. As an honor of their hard work and sacrifice, I later bought the sixty acre tract that contained the site of my birth. My elder daughter, Renee Ryan, bought it from me when I moved to Los Angeles, California in 2003, so it remains in my family until this day. The old sharecropper shack had been torn down by then, but the evidence of its existence remained. It symbolizes a sense of connection between the generations, a stronghold connecting our family lines. It invites us to explore a story that was written long ago, but continues to unfold.

When I think about the home I constructed on our family land, I can't help but think about our first family home. My grandfather, August Long lived in the largest house in our community, but, if I don't describe it, you will have no clue as to how this "big house," that we kids loved so well, was constructed. In fact, you will be astounded as to what we called "great living." When my grandfather moved from the Little River Bottoms and constructed his house up in the "Two Mile Community," the original structure was built out of logs. I remember it well. As the family grew and prospered, rooms were gradually added unto the log house in stages. These rooms were all constructed out of milled lumber. The first room constructed was the kitchen. It was a separate room built next to the log house. When you went to the kitchen you had to walk out of the main house to an open porch-like area which had no top or sides. We had to walk across what we called the "gallery" and into the kitchen. I can still see us in the winter time swiftly running across that gallery.

Later, a series of bedrooms were added to the other side of the main house. And, as I close my eyes and count, it was either four or five bedrooms, with a screened in porch running along three of them. All of these were constructed out of milled lumber and built by my grandfather's sons. Several of the bedrooms were built higher off the ground than the others, which turned out to be great for us kids, because that is where we loved to play during the heat of the summer, under the house in the sand. However, hopefully, you did not have to go to the "bathroom" in bad or cold weather, because that was a big hole in the ground where they placed small wood over a concrete bottom with holes that you could sit on as you used the bathroom. Because of the continual foul odor that came from this little room, it was necessary to place it anywhere from twenty five to fifty yards from the house. Oh such memories of home!

My health during early childhood

My early childhood was rift with many health problems. On two different occasions the doctors told my mother to take me home because I only had a few days to live. My mother had already lost her child, Robert Lee Swift, shortly after he was born. I can only imagine the pain that darkened my mother's spirit to lose a part of her soul. He was a helpless child that she could not protect. There were no ancestral wisdoms, no tribunal ceremonies that could spare him, so my mother, who was quite a fighter, had no intentions of losing any other children without a fight. I believe that is the reason that as I write this letter, all nine of us who survived childbirth are still alive.

When I was four, I became very sick. This was the second time my frail health was challenged. During this health scare I had pneumonia and was hospitalized. My mother would visit me daily. One night she feared I would not make it throughout the night so she stayed by my side. Several doctors were on tour that night looking over the facility and one of the doctors saw Mama sleeping on the hard and cold floor. The doctor said, "Why is she sleeping on that floor?" He was a stranger to the area and didn't fully understand the treatment we had to endure. He told someone to get her a bed to sleep in and Mama said it wasn't long before she heard a bed being rolled into the room for her. The second time I became ill, my mother and grandmother, Lugrelia Long, took me to the office of a Dr. Swift in Cameron, Texas. I think my grandmother was some kind of "Don Quixote" the Spanish knight who was always fighting windmills and Dr. Swift's staff was my grandmother's windmills. They always insisted on spelling my last name as "SMITH" rather than the doctor's last name which was "SWIFT". My grandmother would be incensed at their inability to recognize that this little black baby's name could be the same as his white, established and successful doctor. It would not only show on her face, but in her tone of voice as well. Her silent strength and the deepened creases in her face clearly spoke her displeasure. What our name represented to them I do not know, nor did my mother or grandmother care.

Each time this happened my grandmother went into a tirade, insisting they spell my last name correctly. I think that this battle only concluded when I got well enough to stop going to Dr. Swift. But during this visit to his office my mother and grandmother had greater concern, my health. Dr. Swift told my mother that I had "double pneumonia, and I would probably live only two or three days. My mother and grandmother began a long and solemn journey as they took me home in silence. This was in December of 1939 and my mother was heavy with child and my sister Betty was only a year old. You can imagine the stress this must have put her through. Both she and my grandmother were saddened at the thought of losing another child (my brother Robert died shortly after birth) and my mother could not fathom living through another loss. Suddenly my grandmother fought back her tears and broke the silence as she remembered something Grandma Saddlewhite told her about an old Indian remedy.

When they arrived home they went into the woods near the Long Mountain and dug up roots and herbs to make tea. I think I know the name of this plant, but I will not say. Mama said they sat back and prayed for a miracle. The roots of this plant were chopped up finely and boiled into a tea which they fed to me. I fought mightily to keep from drinking the foul tasting tea and every time I spit it out, Mama and my grandmother would force more into my mouth. They were relieved when eventually, after much fighting, I surrendered.

Although the women in my family surrounded me with their prayers and were hopeful, I was so sick my Aunt Odessa thought I would never have another Christmas. She picked up my frail body and took me into the hearth room where the family Christmas tree was and stood there for me to see it. Then she carried me back to my bed. They continued walking, pacing, fearful and hoping, as though to will me back to life. Mama, both of my grandmothers and aunts stood guard over me around the clock,. I vaguely remember this time because as I began to get well, every time I wanted something to eat they would feed me crackers and peppermint candy which helped soothe the lingering taste in my mouth. Three days of their nursing me and the power of healing from nature was all that was needed. My mother said they took great pleasure in taking me back to the Dr. Swift so he could see that I was fully recovered.

My mother, Juanita Swift

3

THE COTTON FIELD WORKER

I learned to walk as my mother worked in the cotton fields. Cotton pickers had to return to work and either carry their infants on their backs or lay them down as they worked and watch them from afar. In the humid heat, neither were optimal conditions, but my mother knew she had no choice but to keep me near her. As I got older and my sibling count began to grow, we too learned how to contribute. As you grew into size and strength enough to work, small children were giving the task of sweeping, picking cotton or carrying water. Early on I was introduced to my own personal cotton sack, made from a burlap bag. Even though I was very young at the time I still remember the sense of pride I felt because I was helping the family make a living. Later I was able to chop cotton in the area cotton fields for thirty cents an hour working ten hours a day Monday through Friday and able to earn fifteen dollars a week!

In the fall of each year my mother and I along with other friends, family members and neighbors, would be hauled by a contractor to the cotton fields of northwest Texas to work in the fields near cities such as Lubbock, Amarillo, Levelland, Tahoka, Big

Springs and Post. There we would get paid fifty cents an hour and were allowed to work six ten hour days, and make THIRTY DOLLARS A WEEK! We would then return back home to Central Texas and prepare to begin picking cotton. I took much pride in having my own money and being able to make an essential contribution and add value to the family household.

One day I took sick on the cotton field and the next day I could not go to the field. I was in agony the entire day that my mother and siblings were working and I could not contribute. When the family returned home after a long day's work, Mama saw that I was not better and had difficulty walking. She took me to the hospital and found that I had appendicitis and needed surgery. That was the second serious type of illness I had. In those days there were no phones, no lights, no cars, just an anxious mother with her six children and a seriously sick child. Somehow, Mama found someone to get me to the hospital. I imagine that once again, my frail health was cause for much stress to my mother. I marvel now at the awesomeness of GOD and his ability to shield and take care of you in woeful times. As I say that I'm thinking of his ability to take care of my mother emotionally because I am sure in the back of her mind she was once again afraid that she would lose a child, but her strength as a mother was of paramount importance.

Picking cotton – A family affair

In Central Texas we "picked" cotton. We would pluck the cotton lint from the boils, therefore, the cotton you placed in your sack was generally very clean. As I got to be older, maybe at the age of 12, I could pick approximately 200 pounds of cotton per day. The heat of the sun would scorch our skin and the boiling sweat that poured down our brows would sting as they hit the heaviness of our drenched shirts. It was a back breaking job and I hated seeing my mother moving slowly down each cotton row. I noticed the slight contrast of her dark callused hands against her brown skin as she picked cotton. I worked alongside of her day by day and she never complained as she earned an honest day of pay. As Mama picked cotton, the older four children went too. When she was not pregnant, we still went to pick along with Cousin Dick as our overseer, which was a bad mistake, especially for Betty, Edgar and Jessie, because he liked to hit them. I was older and on my own picking cotton.

One day I was caught by Cousin Dick or another overseer as I tried to "sneak" a little clod of dirt here and a little clod of dirt there to increase the weight in my cotton sack. Although I knew it was wrong, I didn't realize it was stealing. I told myself that if I brought home more money I could better help support my family. Honorable as that may seem I don't know now if that was my true intention at the time. What I was doing was stealing. By the time they finished with me, I decided stealing or cheating was never going to be in my best interest.

At two dollars per hundred pounds, I was making four dollars each day to pick cotton in Central Texas. It was ten hours of hard work in the unrelenting hot Texas sun. Even now as I travel in the western states and see the migrant workers harvesting the fields I am sympathetic because I know and understand what they are going through to make a decent living. It takes my mind to the many days the heat would be so intense in the cotton fields that we tried to walk with our feet underneath the cotton stalks hiding them from the sun to keep them cool. Sometimes that worked and many times it did not.

After we finished picking the cotton in Central Texas, we loaded up and moved back to West Texas to begin to harvest the cotton crops. There they grew a different kind of cotton, by the time we got there to harvest, their cotton stalks were much smaller and the cotton plants were much drier. Instead of picking cotton as we did in Central Texas, in West Texas we "pulled" cotton. That meant that you could take both hands and reach down to the bottom of the stalk and "pull up," bringing up dry leaves and other debris along with the cotton lint. The cotton harvested in this fashion was much dirtier than the picked cotton and you could "pull" a considerable amount more cotton than you could pick. I worked hard and fast and as a twelve year old kid I could pull approximately four hundred pounds of cotton each day. The price we made for harvesting this way was still approximately two dollars per hundred. I could make eight dollars a day, work six full days each week and bring home forty eight dollars a week! It is little wonder why many moved to West Texas and never returned to Central Texas again. I have many of my generation that I grew up and went to school with still living in West Texas.

The Swift family income from us working in the cotton fields greatly supplements my daddy's income and I was proud to make my contribution. In fact, the "Swift Kids" never complained about

4

SCHOOL DAYS

By the time my family finished working in the fields, it was October before I finally got an opportunity to attend school. Of course, that was not the way it was prior to me getting large enough to go to work full time. Going to school was a luxury every family could not afford. But as a child I attended the little "Two Mile" school which taught the first through the eighth grade. It had been that way since my mother and my father attended this same school many eons before. I often wondered when I sat in class the difference between the school when I attended and when my mother attended it as a child. I wondered about the similarities and the differences. In my parents early days they didn't attend formal school because there was none for colored children. When they opened the one room Two Mile School for the colored children to attend, my parents were able to gain their education. It wasn't easy for them, as their responsibility to help support their family was much greater than the demands in my day. And the added stress of the continued slave mentality of not only white society, but also of blacks, kept them from branching out to explore their full potential. When my siblings and I were in school, the atmosphere although similar, was beginning to change. At a recent reunion of the Two Mile Negro School, attendees were able to reminisce about the field trips that were taken to Sugarloaf Mountain, over the hill to the Smith Bottom and dipping vat on our property. We recalled the dedicated teachers that guided us and shared great memories. Two Mile Negro School closed in 1951 and has been demolished.

I don't remember much except that I was very good at spelling. Weekly, the teacher would line all of us from the sixth through the eighth grade to have an old fashion spelling bee. If someone ahead of you misspelled a word, the student who spelled it correctly was moved up the line towards the head. I loved being at the head of the line and worked hard to stay there. As a tall child I would tower over some of the older children which gave me a sense of determination that I needed to perform at their level. I believed I should be able to spell the words the children my age and older children could spell. That was my motivation.

It was not unusual for other things to take priority over education for the blacks in the South. Although the black middle class was emerging in the northern states and the literacy levels of black children was rising throughout the country, education for southern rural blacks was simply for you to receive a minimum education of the basic three "R's" of Reading, "Riting" and "Rithmetic." This would prepare you for the menial tasks that it was anticipated you would do. If we wanted to get additional schooling it was necessary that the family made arrangements to go to the Black School in Gause, Texas, approximately three miles from where my family lived, where they also taught the ninth and tenth grade. However, when my mother was attending school, if you wanted to graduate from a high school it was necessary for your family to make arrangements for the student to live with a family in whatever town you chose. The closest black high school that you could receive a diploma from was twenty three miles away in Cameron, Texas. My mother, Juanita Long Swift, had to go almost a hundred miles away to a town called "Red Lands" where she received her high school diploma. Since the ability to attend high school was a novelty, most blacks were thrilled to have the free education for their children and them living in a different city was a small sacrifice. Because many whites did not want black children to become educated, the schools had fewer books and learning resources than those of the white schools.

This discrimination continued throughout my early learning years. I believe this was an attempt to keep us working in the fields or as domestic service workers. Although the strategy worked, the self-opposed inferiority stigma was beginning to decrease and the desire of blacks in the South to expand their educational opportunities was becoming more important. I thank my parents for identifying the importance of education for their children and I believe it set the foundation for my desire to continue my education, even today.

Education was important to both parents but I think that Daddy wanted more for us than Mama due to the fact that Daddy only went to the third grade in school. He also attended Two Mile Negro School and in later years continued his education. In Mama's case, she had witnessed how hard Granddaddy worked to send his first child, Aunt Ida, to school and she didn't use her education. She earned her sheepskin from Paul Quinn in Waco, Texas. Mama always told us that we had to get our education, but would have to attend college on our own, and her word stood. Most of the time, if you asked Daddy for money for something that enhanced your education he would provide it. As a side note, my dad was a cool kind of guy. He loved his daughters and they loved him. They would climb all over him and he would hug and kiss them, but he did not outwardly show love toward the boys. I recall telling my children that I never recall him telling me he loved me as a young child or adult. Finally as an adult I grabbed him one day and embraced him and said, "I love you." It was a very awkward moment, but it was what I needed. From then on, I began hugging Daddy every time I saw him and I got the point across that boys like hugs from their father too. Daddy had no choice but to give in to my hugs. That's why I'm affectionate with my kids and I tell them constantly thru words and thru deeds that I love them. Children need to know that.

My father, Leroy Swift, Sr.

5

A MAN OF CHARACTER

During World War II, my father, Leroy Swift Sr., wanted to serve in the United States Army. He was a very loyal and patriotic man, and wanted to do his part. When he went to volunteer his service he was rejected because he already had four children. But my father was undaunted by the rejection. Instead, he was determined to do his part. He was told that he could sit out the war and serve his country better by working in one of the many defense plants that was located in Texas. That was just not good enough for him. He wanted to make a difference!.

Finally, my father heard about a huge army camp that was being constructed near Killeen, Texas, which was less than one hundred miles from where we lived. My dad, being a very persistent person, packed his bags and headed for Killeen!! He again tried to join the army, and after being rejected he went to   work   at   this large army camp called "Camp Hood." It was never clear to me as to what exactly he did, but I remember as a little kid listening to him tell mama about all of the exciting things he was doing. Looking back I am sure that whatever he was doing was more exciting than plowing behind a team of mules as I watched.

Little did I realize that what my father was doing, they were in fact, building the military base that would ultimately become Fort Hood, the largest military base in the world. At some point, as near as I can remember, my father was promoted to a supervisory position and transferred to another army camp that was being constructed in Texas. It was, and remains to this day, Camp Swift. I am not sure of the origin of this SWIFT name, but listening to Daddy you would have thought it was named after him!

There were many things that my father taught me that has served me well throughout my life. He was, first of all, the "provider" for our family. He would work any and all kinds of jobs to make sure that his family was fed and housed properly. Though he was not much of a carpenter, he even built a house for us to live in when we moved to Houston, Texas. It certainly was not fancy, but it was definitely functional.

My father had strong mental, as well as physical strength and could hold his own alongside the best of men in any endeavor. If I had to use one word to describe him I would describe him as a "hustler". I am sure some of my siblings might take issue with that description, but I learned to "hustle" right along beside him! That was one of the reasons the SWIFT family was never hungry and always had a roof over our heads. I never forgot that, consequently my family never went hungry and always had a roof over their heads. My daddy was not a learned man having only completed the third grade before he had to quit school to take care of his mother and siblings. Nevertheless, as long as he lived in the country, I still remember him going to night school at the old Black Two Mile

School. He continued to study there until he obtained the equivalent of a seventh grade education. Yes, I thought it was kind of funny, that my daddy was going to "my" school at night. I remember mama taking me to the schoolhouse some nights watching daddy as he worked in class. He never stopped trying to better himself!

My father's work ethic was such that he would try anything that he saw anybody else do to make a living. I would say that he was a "jack of all trades," and master of none. Not only did he own and operate a very profitable trucking firm beginning in 1948-49, which he ultimately expanded to eight trucks, he also at various and sundry times

- sold cars
- operated a filling station
- operated a family restaurant, ran a.
- trash hauling service

Even when my daddy was past 80 years old he was still experimenting with ways to make another dollar. I know, because from time to time he would call me and ask me what I thought. I had to be very careful with my responses, because what I wanted to tell him was to just "cool it" and enjoy what you have, but that simply was not in him.

Why am I telling my kids this? My daddy taught me to persevere. To never give up until you accomplish what you set out to do. I am saying that you are my daddy's descendants, and somewhere in your paternal DNA there should be some of what I call "stick to it ness", that you should have to make you "keep on keeping on". That will be the legacy my father left us.

My grandfather, August Long

6

THE JOURNEY BEGINS

My grandfather, we called him Granddaddy, was one of the deacons at the small country church which most of my family were members of. It was called the Mount Tabor Baptist Church. This church's predecessor had begun during slavery time in the Little River Bottoms and was located at the foot of a small mountain peak near Gause, Texas which the locals called the Sugar Loaf Mountain. There was a sense of beauty in the land that still remains. The rolling hills that appear as a carpet of mossy green landscape rose above the fertile valley that lay at its feet. You can then understand why later many of the former slaves, including my family, became sharecroppers and continued to live and work the lands where they had previously served as slaves.

After slavery was abolished, (which the central Texas slaves found out about two years later, hence our Juneteenth celebrations in Texas) the black sharecroppers named their church the Black Israelite Church. As the black sharecroppers began to shift about and move away from the Little River Bottoms, it was necessary for the church to follow the population shift. As blacks began to purchase land on the hills above the Little River Bottom, the Black Israelite Church closed due to failing membership.

During the 1880's the church at the foot of Sugar Loaf Mountain closed and the congregation split and formed two new churches. One of the congregations became the Zion Hill Baptist Church and moved to the township of Gause, Texas. The second congregation from the Black Israelite Church was formed of those members who continued to live and work in the Little River Bottoms. It was relocated to property that had been owned by my great-grandfather, Elbert Long, and had been passed on to my grandfather when his father passed. This property was located at the foot hills of the Little River Bottoms, near the township of Gause.

August Long, along with the members, named their new church the Mount Tabor Baptist Church. Later, around 1927, as members continued to leave the Bottoms, Mount Tabor was moved again. This time on top of the hills of the Little River Bottoms to an area called the Two Mile Community of Gause, Texas. The elders understood the role that Mount Tabor played in maintaining our community. The culturally distinct way in which we worshiped as a black family and community created a unique and empowering stronghold in many families, so it was important that those in the area had a place of comfort, a church home. The praise and worship of the congregation served as a fueling station for many, helping us live thru the struggles and the disenfranchisement we endured. My grandfather and the other elders in the church felt strongly that the church was and should be the center of our community. Granddaddy remained a prime mover in the affairs of the Two Mile Community, as well as the Mount Tabor Baptist church where he served as a Deacon and Sunday School Superintendent, and it went without saying that his children and grandchildren would be in attendance.

25

My Maternal Grandfather's influence on my life

I was told by my aunties that even at the age of 4-5 I was my grandfather's shadow. When he walked the dusty (or muddy) road to church with his bible under his arm, I walked right along behind him with a book under my arm. I still remember the excitement that I felt when he finally allowed me to carry his bible for him. It was almost like a "rite of passage". Oh how I loved that man! It is no doubt that even as I pen these words at the age of seventy four (I will be 75 in August), my maternal grandfather, August "Gus" Long, has been "THE" major role model in my life. I am sure that his influence shaped my life for the years to come, especially my walk with Christ today.

In our small rural community, he was always the "go to" person if you had a need for anything. If people in the community did not have any milk cows, all they had to do was tell Granddaddy. He would select a cow from his herd and they would come over and milk it each morning. For those that were too old or not feeling well, I would be assigned to milk the cow and take the milk to you. One day when he told me to milk an elderly neighbor's cow and take the milk to her, I made the mistake of complaining. My grandfather quickly corrected my attitude and I NEVER EVER complained again about any assignment he gave me. When he killed hogs, or cows, he always butchered enough for the whole community! Being close to my grandfather, I even remember having to go out during the cold weather and load up a wagon full of wood and take it to anyone who was in need. That kind of giving was prevalent in all aspects of our community. My grandfather had that giving and caring spirit until he was in his late eighties. Oh, how he loved to serve his community.

With my grandfather, just to be in his presence was an awesome experience for me. My auntie kids me even today, about how much I strived as a kid to imitate him. She recounts that when I was a little kid my grandfather would come out of the fields at noon and lie down on his day bed and read the Bible or newspaper. When he did this my grandfather would cross his legs in a very peculiar way. When family members would drop by his favorite spot where he would be reading or taking his mid-day siesta, they would find me lying next to him with a book, many times holding it upside down, "reading" with my legs crossed like my granddaddy! It's truly amazing how some people come into your life for a season and have a permanent positive influence on who you are or will become.

As I mentioned earlier, my grandfather was also the Sunday School Superintendent, as well as the primary teacher. We had Sunday School every Sunday except when there was a fifth Sunday in the month. On those Sundays there was generally some kind of special service or activity at one of the churches in the area and other churches would join them in fellowship. I recall it being each fourth Sunday that the circuit preacher came to our church and preached a sermon, (and ate up my grandmother's fried chicken, much to my consternation). On each Sunday he would rotate and go to a different church. Since the circuit preacher did not live in our area, we only saw him once a month unless there was a funeral or wedding he had to officiate. If we could not get the circuit preacher, my Grandfather or one of the other Deacons would handle the services.

Oh, I thank God for the Godly and God fearing role model he provided for me, and I am so mindful today as the grandfather of over thirty grandkids, how important it is for us to provide a Godly image, a Godly pattern for our offsprings to emulate. Our children "see" and "hear" everything we "do" and "say" in their presence. If it is good, they remember it. If it is bad, they remember that also. Emulating the Christian man, my maternal grandfather, has brought me a very long ways in my life. He taught me how to love all people and to strive to serve them, and not be judgmental. Maybe that was the beginning of this odyssey, my walk with Christ.

My early church days

When I turned 12 years old, along with several other young children, I was baptized at Mount Tabor at the old water tank where we watered my grandfather's cattle. I look back on my past and sometimes ask myself, *"what was the purpose of that baptism?"* I did not know very much about Jesus Christ, who much later became my Lord and Savior, nor did I have any special feelings or revelation concerning Him. I was baptized because everyone else was being baptized and I did not want to be left out. Back then the "old folk" would also insist that you be baptized when you reached a certain age. They felt that if you were from a Christian family, this was the proper thing to do and that it led to your salvation. Even though I had no desire, it was easier just to comply. So I did.

The reason I am dwelling on the origin of Mount Tabor and the influence of my grandfather, is because I believe that those early influences on my life, especially that one man, my grandfather, in so many ways is the reason that I am who I am today and the reason that I now am the Pastor of Mount Tabor Baptist Church, my grandfather's old church.

7

FAMILY TIES

My grandfather August Long's father was named Elbert Long. During slavery he was sold by the Major Long family, who lived on the Eastern Shores of the State of Maryland, to an Alabama slave owner whose last name was Hannah, (possibly spelled Hanna). The Hannah family, including Grandpa Elbert, later moved to Central Texas with their slaves. I am told that Grandpa Elbert was one of the slaves responsible for working inside of the home as a personal servant and was not accustomed to working outside in the fields. As a house slave, he lived better than the field slaves, but this in no way gave him an easy life.

According to my mother, the new slave owner, Master Hannah, considered Grandpa Elbert, who I am told was a well built and very distinguished looking man, to be better equipped to serve as a field hand and he was placed in that role. Grandpa Elbert hated serving in that capacity and subsequently ran away. He was later captured by runaway slave hunters and returned to the Hannah family.

As punishment, as an example and to bring shame, the head of the Hannah family decided to whip him in front of all of his slaves. He was stripped naked, his hands were tied and he was beaten with a whip. My grandpa, August Long, said that he was told that Grandpa Elbert refused to flinch even though the owner beat him unmercifully. Finally, the owner's mother asked her son to stop and to give Grandpa Elbert to her to be used as her personal servant.

Grandpa Elbert spent the remainder of slavery years working back inside of the Hannah home, serving in the various capacities that required his attention. After slavery was abolished, Grandpa Elbert refused to take the last name of Hannah, instead choosing the last name of "Long" from his family's previous owner.

During this period, through means unknown to me, Grandpa Elbert received a fairly decent education. He became an avid supporter of his offsprings obtaining as much education as possible. That trait continues to be prominent in the Long family offsprings, even until this day.

As a freedman, Elbert Long began to amass a large number of acreage in Milam County, Texas. His land holdings extended from the Little River to what is now US Highway 79. I am told that one of the mysteries was how Grandpa Elbert was always able to come up with the large amounts of money that he needed whenever his land payments were due. I even remember going back and searching various records to come up with a clue. I could see by the county records that he always paid his taxes and mortgage payments on time. But, considering the large amount of money he needed to pay his obligations, I could not figure out where the money came from.

Years later, two of my old aunts explained the mystery. Grandpa Elbert was a personal friend of Sam Bass, the young and notorious Texas train and bank robber! Sam Bass was orphaned at 13 and left Mississippi and moved to Denton, Texas where he took up horse racing. Eventually he drove cattle from San Antonio north and was to give the owner $8,000. But instead of returning the $8,000 to the owners in Texas, he and his partners took off, gambling and squandering the money. By 1878 he was robbing stage coaches and trains, which resulted in a pursuit by citizens. I recalled studying about the fact that Sam Bass and his gang would elude capture when they would be working in the Texas area, and law enforcement authorities were puzzled because they would often just "disappear." They never could find Sam Bass and his gang.

My aunties said that Sam Bass and his gang would hide out on Grandpa Elbert's farm down in the Little River Bottoms. It seems as though he would come to this black man's place and hide out behind the small hill that we call the "Long Mountain," in a heavily wooded area. Nobody thought to look for him in that area. Apparently he kept a cache of money there, which Grandpa Elbert had access to. Eventually the Texas Rangers caught up to him in Round Rock in 1878 and fatally wounded him. He was twenty seven. Grandpa Elbert Long died in the late 1880s.

The admission by my aunties of the connection Grandpa Elbert had with Sam Bass explained another mystery to me. When I was a little boy I remembered that somehow Granddaddy had gotten in arrears on his property taxes and without letting him know, the County sheriff had scheduled to have his land sold on the steps of the Milam County court house. All of these arrangements had been made in an under-handed fashion, without my grandfather's notification. All of this makes sense if you realize that Granddaddy held some very choice pieces of land and the local farmers had been trying to buy this land for many years.

When the County Judge, a man by the last name of Ely who was a fair and upright man, found out about the Sheriff's sale, he sent notice for my grandfather to appear in his office just prior to the sale and did not let anyone know that he was coming. I clearly remember that Granddaddy was told to come to the County Judge's officer through a back way - I was there. Here is the part that got me. Granddaddy saddled up his horse, Old Dan, and told the family that he had to go to the "Bottoms." I wanted to go and did not mind walking behind Granddaddy while he rode his horse.

Granddaddy told me to stay home and rode off. Several hours later he returned with a burlap sack tied to his saddle horn. When he opened it we found that he was carrying a lot of what we called back then, "Bo Dollars" which were the old U.S silver dollars. Granddaddy showed up at the County Judge's office the next day before noon and paid his taxes.

A large number of farm owners gathered at the court house sale waiting to bid on his land. The County Judge waited until just a few minutes before the sale was to begin when he stepped out and advised the crowd that the taxes had been paid in full! Both Granddaddy and the County Judge were somewhat amused by the consternation of the awaiting bidders as this choice land had slipped through their hands. We still own 480 acres of that land today!

Marcus Shepard's drawing of Great Grandma Rebecca
Saddlewhite and my Grandfather August Long

Original photo of Great Grandmother Rebecca Saddlewhite and
my Grandfather, August Long

My great grandmother, Rebecca Saddlewhite, was Granddaddy's mother. She lived with him until she died in 1917. I remember watching the picture of Grandmother Saddlewhite, my grandfather, August Long and my Uncle Bennie Long, that my nephew Marcus Shepard, who is an awesome artist, drew for my 60th birthday. I love that picture and had it mounted in my living room above the fireplace.

Studying that picture one day, and seeing Grandma Saddlewhite standing there looking like an old Indian squaw, I began to wonder about the Choctaw Indians, whose blood coursed through the Long family's veins. I remember the oral history what my mother shared with us concerning Grandma Saddlewhite's mother, who was a slave that was "loaned" by her owner to a Choctaw Indian which we were taught to call Chief Saddlewhite. This Indian Chief had been a friend of her parents and it turned out that she was to be one of Chief Saddlewhite's slaves or concubines.

Subsequently, Grandma Rebecca was born to Chief Saddlewhite and my Great-great grandmother. Later Grandma Rebecca's mother was returned to her original slave owner where I lost track of her. This means that if Great-grandmother was 1/2th Choctaw, then my grandfather, August Long would have been 1/4th Choctaw, my mother, Juanita Long would have been 1/8th Choctaw, and I would be 1/16th Choctaw. WOW! As you will see later, that is not all of the Indian blood that we have running through our veins.

I remember my grandfather talking about the horrible scars that his mother had on her back and neck from the relentless beatings she endured with whips. She apparently resisted vigorously at men's attempts to abuse her. My grandfather said that when the weather changed, the scars on his mother's back became so painful that he had to take "tallow" and rub it over her to alleviate the pain. He said that he had to pray to keep from hating all white men because of what they did to his mother. God answered his prayers because he hated no man. The hate that he had for the white men who unmercifully beat and abused his mother was gone. That was a significant lesson my granddaddy taught me - that there should be no room in a Christian's heart for hate. I never forgot that "sweetness" that he had in his spirit.

When Grandma Saddlewhite married Grandpa Elbert, both of them already had one child. Grandpa Elbert had a daughter whose name was Lytha. We are all familiar with her off-spring because she married Peter Brown whose family land is adjacent to ours. Our cousin Curtis Terrell is a part of that lineage. Grandma Saddlewhite had a son who was very fair in complexion and had straight hair. His name was Albert. He also possessed distinct white features. When slavery ended Albert was taken from Grandma Saddlewhite by some white men to never be seen again.

Albert, being forcibly taken away from Grandma Saddlewhite, may have a bearing on an incident that happened to me back around 1996-97. I was living in the new retirement home that I had constructed on my farm on Long Mountain Road. One day I was working in one of my hay fields and a white man and woman drove up to me and asked if I knew of any "Longs" living in the area. I made the silly comment, "this must be your lucky day, my name is Swift but I am a descendant of the Long family."

This man seemed to get excited and asked me if I ever heard of a man named Elbert Long. I told him that was my grandfather's name. He said to me that in his research he found that he had Negro blood in him and he was trying to locate the grave of Elbert Long. I explained to him that Elbert Long was buried in the Old Black Israelite Church cemetery and that none of us knew where that cemetery was located, except somewhere at the foot of Sugar Loaf Mountain. All of that local area has now been reclaimed by tree growth. I sent the man off to find my cousin and I never got the chance to see him again. I had many questions to ask him.

My Paternal Grandfather – And his bride

I never knew my daddy's father, John Swift, since he died before I was born. But I heard so many stories about him from my father, his sisters and old friends. There is an interesting similarity between my maternal grandfather's last name of Long, and my paternal grandfather's last name of Swift. After slavery, in most cases, the names of our African ancestors had been removed from our forefather's memories. It was then the custom when slaves were freed that they assumed the last name of their previous owner. Elbert Long hated his new master, whose last name was Hannah, so much that he refused to use his last name after he was freed. Before he was sold to the Hannah's, the family of Elbert belonged to a slave owner on the Eastern shores of Maryland. This owner's name was Major Long, so Elbert took that name instead.

In the case of Grandpa John Swift, his family was slaves in the vicinity of Atlanta, Georgia. After he supposedly killed a man, he fled for his life. My daddy said that his last name had been Spurgeon or a similar sounding name, when he lived in Georgia. But Grandpa John changed his last name to Swift to prevent anyone from finding him.

As soon as I retired from the Kansas City Missouri Police Department, I felt a sense of urgency to do some research on him before all of the people who knew him would pass away. Almost everyone I spoke to talked about how "strange" he was. His daughter, Aunt Jessie Lee, said that her father did not sleep in a bed until just a few months before he died at the age of 87. She said that he slept fully dressed sitting in a rocking chair by his bed. When the weather was nice he always went into the wood near Aunt Jessie Lee's house, and his dog went with him. She said that he always slept in the trees. Sometimes very late at night she would hear a loud noise coming from the woods near her house, which was her father's way of letting her know that he was okay. Through interviews I discovered that Grandpa John Swift was still sleeping out in the woods up in trees at night, until he was in his upper 70s. Aunt Jessie Lee said that if anything came close to grandpa, the dog would begin barking and wake him up. Many times grandpa would be sleeping so close to the house that she could hear his dog bark.

My father explained to me that Grandpa John was a light complexioned "red-bone" man. His skin color was due to the fact that he was one half Indian and one half Black. When I asked my father which Indian tribe we were related to through Grandpa John, he said that he was not absolutely sure. Of course, I finally discovered that Grandpa John Swift was one-half Cherokee Indian and one-half African.

Grandpa John had been married and had a family when he lived in Georgia near Atlanta. At some point my grandfather had gotten into some kind of fight and killed one or two men in the State of Georgia where he was born. He then fled for his life. Grandpa John decided that he wanted to get far enough from Georgia so the authorities would not be able to find him. He finally ended up in the State of Texas. The first indication of Grandpa John Swift being in the state of Texas was when he showed up at a plantation in Old Washington County where the City of Navasota was located at the time. Grandpa John was in his early forties and had apparently been imprisoned here in Texas and was working out his sentence on a prison chain gang. The prison chain gang had been hired to work on the Allen Plantation. That was where the family of the young woman who was destined to be my paternal grandmother lived and worked.

My future grandma was named Vader Hilliard and was fourteen years old. Some kind of way Grandpa John, my forty something year old grandfather, and that fourteen year old "child," made a connection. And one night after he finished his prison sentence, Grandma Vader simply disappeared. Nobody seemed to know what happen to her. When others asked the family about her location, they would say "she is lost." In fact, I am told that over the years the family always referred to her as "Lost Vader."

Years later, when all of the facts were pieced together, we learned what happened. When Grandpa John finished his prison term, he showed up at the Allen Plantation in the middle of the night and took Grandma Vader to Hearne, Texas to a place along the Little Brazos River. In my research, I was able to locate a marriage license for Grandpa John and Grandma Vader at the Robertson County courthouse in Franklin, Texas. It listed grandpa's age as forty-seven and grandma's age as fifteen. (Keep in mind that John Swift was still married to a wife back in Georgia.)

Grandpa John and Grandma Vader had grown children before any of her family found out that she was still alive. It seems as though Grandpa John and his family were working as sharecroppers on the same farm near Gause that Mr. Calvin Moore and his wife Alice worked. My grandma and Mrs. Alice were great friends, and looking back in my mind, they could have almost passed for twins. Neither one of them weighed more than 90 pounds soaking wet and they both dipped snuff, which I hated. One day

Mrs. Alice's father came to visit her. During the visit he met his daughter's friend Vader. Noticing the resemblance, he asked Grandma Vader where she was from and what her maiden name was. When grandma answered her friend's father, he just broke down and wept. He kept mumbling, "I have found lost Vader, I have found lost Vader". It was not until that time that Grandma Vader and the Hilliards, her family were united. For more than twenty years she lived within a fifty mile radius of her family.

Grandma Vader was a little tiny woman, yet two or three of her boys were very big, powerfully built men weighing three to four hundred pounds. I think that overall she and Grandpa John had seven boys and five girls. My father was a nice two hundred pound man, but I think that it was those "Swift" genes which caused me to weigh in at three hundred pounds for a while when I was working at the Kansas City Missouri police department. In my 70s I manage to keep my weight in the two hundred and forty pound range.

When Grandpa John's children were teenagers, he decided it was time to go back to Georgia and check on his original family. He had a wife and some children there as well and he longed to see them. The story is told that in the spring of that year, Grandpa John was chopping in the Little River Bottoms when he came to the end of his row. He stuck his hoe upright in the soil and stepped into the adjacent woods. The rest of the choppers thought, as was the custom, he was going to use the bathroom. Nobody saw or heard from him for a year and a half. One fall day while everyone was gathering in the cotton, they looked up and saw this man coming out of the woods. IT WAS GRANDPA JOHN! Somehow he had worked his way back to Georgia and visited with his family. Nothing was ever said about his absence from either of his families. I asked my daughter, Darrylyn, to research the Swift family in

Georgia.   Although she made a few connections, the search continues.

Grandma Vater Swift

8

A NEW LIFE

In 1949 my life entered into a new and exciting season. My parents, Leroy Swift and Juanita Catherine Long-Swift, moved with their eight kids (they later had a ninth) to Houston, Texas. The move was because daddy, who was working at Shelfield Steel running a machine that made carpenter nails, decided that he wanted to go into business for himself. To get started, he purchased a brand new 1949 Dodge one and a half ton stake bed truck with a dump bed. In those days Houston had less than one million population but it was a hustling and bustling waterfront town and Daddy wanted a piece of the action.

Thus the small trucking company, "SWIFT DELIVERY SERVICE" was birthed, which ultimately grew to eight trucks. I remember Daddy bragging about the fact that in his first two days of driving his new truck, he made more money then he made each week at Shelfield Steel, including overtime. Of course at thirteen years of age I had already been driving trucks hauling cotton to the cotton gins in West Texas. No driver's license was required back then because these trucks were considered to be farm trucks.

When we moved to Houston, Daddy immediately took me to get a Texas driver's license and signed documents that he was responsible for my driving. And by the time I was fourteen, I had a Texas Commercial Driver's License. Yep, it was that easy back then. I was immediately put to work each day after school hauling trash that could be easily dumped, like grain husks from the Comet Rice Mills, trash from the downtown Joske's store and bulk cardboard paper boxes from one of the large furniture companies. At fourteen, I was already one of the main Swift family providers.

And my daddy? As I previously shared, he was always a hard worker who believed in taking good care of his large family. Also, when it came to his sons, he was A TIGHT WAD! Let me mention one little antidote, and then I will move on. I must preface this by stating that at heart, my father was a junk man. He could never pass up a piece of metal, abandoned batteries, wire or anything else that he perceived had value. He would always stop and throw whatever it was in to the back of his truck to bring it home and throw it in the junk pile, which was in the front yard of our house. Of course, this was unsettling to my mother and embarrassing to me. But Daddy would always defend his actions by saying, "that stuff is worth a lot of money". Periodically, he would load up some of this junk and haul it somewhere and get rid of it. But, much of the items remained behind because Daddy was always picking up more junk.

One day I asked Daddy for five dollars because I needed it for a class project at school. Daddy reached his hand into his pocket and I could see him thinking as he began rubbing on his money. Remember, I told you that he was a tight wad, at least with his boys (his girls could get anything that they wanted). He finally took his hands out of his pocket and told me that if I wanted five dollars I could take the truck and load up some of that metal junk that was cluttering up the front yard, take it down on Jensen Drive and Clinton Drive and sell it at the junk yard. He followed me out to the pile of junk and pointed out stuff for me to take, and then went back into the house. I saw that Daddy was not going to give me any money so I did as he said. When I got to the junk yard they sorted out the junk that I brought, weighed it and told me to go into the office to get my money. I was thinking well, maybe I will get ten or fifteen dollars for this, so "I" will have a little left over. When I went to the office, the lady gave me sixty dollars, CASH! I was in shock. I went home and handed Daddy the money. He peeled off a five dollar bill and gave it to me. I stood firm waiting and expecting a little bit more. Daddy walked out of the house, got in his pickup and happily drove off. I could tell he was happy because he was whistling as he turned the corner and drove out of sight.

As we settled in to Houston, in 1950 my family and I joined the Saint John Baptist Church on Dowling Avenue. Coming from the country, I saw this church which covered most of a city block as being very large. I had never seen such a massive church building. I very quickly became involved in one of the church's two marching bands and began playing the alto saxophone, and later the baritone horn. I really enjoyed marching and playing in that band. When I close my eyes sometimes I can still hear and see our band as we, on special occasions, marched through the streets of the predominately black Third, Fourth, and Fifth Wards of Houston, Texas playing Christian marching songs such as "Oh When the Saints go Marching In." I also played the baritone horn in the Phyllis Wheatley High School marching band as well as the Alto Sax in its Jazz band.

But why did I attend Saint John Baptist? And what was my walk with Christ during these teenage years? I have two answers. I joined Saint John Baptist church because my mama told me to and because I loved playing music, AND they had all of the pretty young girls in Saint John's "Baptist Young Peoples Union" (BYPU). Don't knock it, I married one of those young pretty girls and all of my children are by her.

As far as my walk with Christ, I did not have one at this time. I simply went to church. Meanwhile, at both Mount Tabor in the country and in Saint John Baptist in Houston, I saw many instances of what we call "hypocrisy" in these churches and it left a very bad taste in my mouth as well as many of the other young people. It was like we were being taught that we young people should "do as we say" and not "do as we do." I decided at that point that I wanted nothing to do with religion.

Not only was church life different in Houston, I will admit that I suffered from quite a shock while transitioning from the little two room school in Gause, Texas with one teacher teaching three to four classes, to a very large multi-story building where I had to attend six classes in six separate rooms, with six separate teachers. After I recovered from the shock of moving to the big city, I began to learn. One of the things that I really enjoyed during the six years that I lived in Houston was the quality education that I received, first at the old Phyllis Wheatley High School, which later became the E. O. Smith Junior High School, and the new Phyllis Wheatley Senior High School from which I graduated from in January 1995.

During this period I had several wonderful male and female teachers, however, one of them still stands out in my mind today more than fifty-five years after I graduated. Just like my grandfather, this teacher had a huge impact on my life which has carried me throughout this journey of mine. I had problems with my math courses during my senior high school years and I became so frustrated that I almost gave up on even trying. By then I had a job driving a truck with my father and was making a decent amount of money working after school. I even considered quitting school. My thoughts were *"what the heck, all I am ever going to be is a truck driver like my daddy anyway"*. And that was not all bad because I enjoyed driving trucks very much. In fact, it was in my blood. My daddy was a truck driver, my uncle was a truck driver, my brother later became a truck driver, and my son Matthew has been an over the road truck car hauler for almost thirty years!

By the grace of God I ended up in a math class taught by a young teacher named Lois Plummer. She had such a gentle reasoning and encouraging way of teaching math. Even though I continued to sit in the rear of the classroom with the rest of the "ruffians", I eventually began to raise my hand when she asked questions. The first time I raised my hand my heart was pounding in my chest and my palms became sweaty with anxiety, but I wanted to participate. I will never forget the day that, in the midst of a very difficult problem, Mrs. Plummer said, "Professor Swift, would you come up here and solve this problem for the class." That day and those words changed my life forever. "Professor Swift", she called me. It was as though Mrs. Plummer looked deeply into my soul and knew that I could do it. She had given me a chance to shine and I have never looked back. I made up my mind that I never wanted to disappoint Mrs. Plummer if she called upon me. The end result was that I studied math like mad and I was always prepared.

With rare exception, I have had enough confidence to take on any chore that I have been given and prevailed. Yes, Mrs. Plummer actualized within me a "can do" spirit that has never left. I wonder how many of today's school teachers have that special gift to truly inspire their students to excel in all that they do.

9

A MILITARY CAREER

In January of 1955, after I graduated from the Phyllis Wheatley High School, I decided to join the U.S. Army before the Korean G.I. bill expired. I joined on January 27, 1955 and went to Fort Bliss, Texas for my basic training. For the next three years, while serving mostly in Germany, I stayed away from any form of religious activity. As I pondered this fact, I recall thinking *why bother*. It was during this time period that I realized that the only reason I went to church in my youth was because it was expected of me. Now, since I am grown up, I will not bother to go anymore, I thought.

I thoroughly enjoyed serving in the U. S. Army. It was there that I began to fully appreciate the magnitude of the first rate education I received at the Phyllis Wheatley High School. I then went down to the recruiting office as soon as I graduated and volunteered with approximately thirty others. We were given a battery of tests and towards the end of the day most of the recruits were sent home and they only asked a select few of us to stay. You can imagine how I felt sitting there waiting to be interviewed by the recruiting sergeant. I FELT LIKE A BIG DUMMY! I knew I had failed. When the recruiting sergeant called me into his office, imagine my surprise when he advised me that I made one of the highest scores.

Later when I got to the Fort Bliss, Texas basic training base they marched approximately two hundred and fifty recruits to a large building and began administering a series of different tests. Again, about halfway through the day, they marched most of the recruits back to their barracks and continued to test the handful of us that remained. One of the tests was a series of "dits" and "dahs." They told me later that this was Morse code. I remember thinking it was one of the most absurd things I had ever done. However, that was simply not the case.

Several days after we finished all of the tests I was called from basic field training and advised that my test scores were high enough to be eligible to attend Officer Candidate School. The Army told me that upon completion I would receive my commission as a 2nd Lieutenant! *Ye gads*, I thought these Army folk had gone crazy. I could not fathom the idea that this little kid from "Two Mile" Texas could lead a platoon of men like the little silly looking 2nd Lieutenant that I had for a platoon leader. Later, I was called back to Battalion Headquarters and asked if I wanted to be a helicopter pilot. Of course, the answer was NO! My mama taught me that if God wanted man to fly he would have given them wings.

I heard so many times back in the 50s and 60s that black men were continually held back from any advancement. Yet, throughout my life I never had that experience. Not in the U. S. military, as you can see, and not in law enforcement as you will see later. What I experienced was that you had to prepare yourself and go after what you wanted. The desire to achieve and the necessary

49

preparations for what you wanted had to come out of your inner beings. Please know that this approach still works today. That is not to say that others didn't experience terrorizing intimidation at the hands of others. However, to succeed I always believed it was necessary to have a determination, a great spiritual strength that refused to believe that I was a victim of society's injustices. And I believe that those who rose up and paved the way for us all to walk a smoother path had that same belief.

After I finished basic training, I was given a two week leave and then sent to Fort Knox, Kentucky for tank training. Let me pause and share two little anecdotes which will give you some idea of race relations in America during this period. The first one occurred while I was in training at Fort Bliss. I was in a company called "Baker Eight" and we lived in five man huts. I was the only black in my hut. One day after a very hard training day, one of my roommates came in and made a derogatory remark about working like a slave. I took offense to what he said and it was clear to everyone that he and I were going to fight. I immediately remembered the way my ancestors were treated as slaves. I thought about how the slave master stripped my great grandfather naked, hung him by his wrists and laid his flesh naked by the cow skin of the whip, beating him until he was streaming with blood. I thought about my ancestors who were raped and beaten by the slave master. And although I thought about my grandfather telling me it was important to hate no man, my emotions were hard to contain.

The other soldiers in our hut separated us and the platoon sergeant was called. Upon his arrival he reprimanded both of us and advised the two of us that he was going to place us on a special assignment. He instructed us to meet him at the company headquarters in full battle gear with our rifles, but with no ammo.

This was a Friday afternoon after we finished working for the week. The rest of the soldiers were able to go on leave but the two of us had to work.

On Friday at 4PM promptly, our sergeant, a little feisty man who was a veteran of the Korean War and had all kind of military and war decorations on his uniform, picked us up in his jeep. He began by making my antagonist, a fellow from Arkansas whose first name was Carroll, and me sit side by side. We were both highly irritated at the sight of each other and our irritation grew as the silent ride continued. He drove out into the desert from El Paseo, Texas and went approximately thirty miles further into the desert until he came to what appeared to be an abandoned gunnery range. He gave each of us some water and enough sandwiches to last two days. His instructions were simple. "Guard this range until I come back on Sunday evening." He then drove away.

Carroll immediately picked up his belongings and moved to one side of the range as I simultaneously moved to the other. It was good that we did not have bullets for our guns so we were in no danger of killing each other, but for sure each wanted nothing to do with other. Can you imagine what kind of sounds emanates from the desert after the sun goes down? There are critters out there that make noises like you never heard before. It was the constant creaky cries of animals of which you do not know. Harsh, low noises came in a steady note with hollow upturns at irregular intervals, and the faintest noises seemed to softly scream a sympathetic warning. Each time we heard one of those noises, Carroll and I drew a little closer together.

We both had, as a part of our combat gear, one half of a tent shelter and it gets very cold out in the desert at night. By midnight on Friday, Carroll and I had put our differences apart, put our two shelter halves together and worked out a game plan as to how we were going to fight those critters if they attacked us. And by the time that our Sergeant picked us up on late Sunday evening, Carroll and I were the best of friends. "That" was the way the U. S. Army handled its racial conflicts back in those days. After that Carroll and I went everywhere together. It was he and I that went to Kansas City, Missouri so I could find my future wife, Pearl. He and I even joined up to go to Fort Knox for Tank Training together. We did not split up until he shipped off to Japan and I shipped off to Germany. Unfortunately, we were never able to contact each other again.

The second incident occurred after we finished our basic training. We were allowed to go home for a few days rest before we started our advanced training in Fort Knox, Kentucky. When it was time to leave, a fellow Houston soldier and a friend of mine made arrangements to travel together to Kentucky. During that time segregation was still rampant in many, if not most, of the southern states. However, one thing that you need to know about interstate travel during that period in 1955 is that if you were traveling "interstate" it was against federal law for anyone to keep you from traveling in any way. That night my friend Bill, who was white, and I caught the train at the Houston train station and rode over to New Orleans. In New Orleans we caught another train that would take us to Fort Knox. When we got to Jacksonville, Mississippi, Bill and I got off the train to stretch our legs while the train hooked on several old antiquated passenger cars which we called cattle cars. When it was time to get back on the train Bill and I headed towards the same car we rode on from New Orleans. As we approached the car we heard a loud voice saying, "Boy, where do you think you are going?" Bear in mind, both Bill and I are in military uniforms. I simply said to the guy that I was getting back on the car that I was on previously. He began to curse me and direct me to the cattle cars they had just hooked up. I recognized two things immediately. This fellow appeared to be almost maniacal and that he was wearing a pistol. I was not anxious for someone to kill Juanita Swift's number one son because he was insisting on his legal rights. A familiar saying swiftly ran thru my mind. It went something like this. . .

He who ups and runs away,
Will live to run another day!

I found myself thinking, *Lord, if you would just get me safely out of Jacksonville, Mississippi, I won't come back.* And even to this day, though I have driven through Jacksonville, Mississippi many times over the years I NEVER stop in Jacksonville, Mississippi except for the one time I had a flat on my RV bus and was forced to stop.

I then told my friend Bill that I did not want any problems so I would comply. Bill tried to intercede but was berated by this wild man also. I asked Bill if he would go back where we were and look out for my duffle bag. He did, and I crawled up inside the cattle car and the train took off. I watched in horror as we stopped along the way and all blacks were directed to these ancient cars with the hard wooden seats, while the whites were permitted to ride on the newer, more comfortable cars. You can imagine how surprised I was about an hour later when I saw Bill struggling down the aisle dragging our two duffle bags.

After I finished my armored training I became a highly qualified member of one of the U.S Army's M-47 tanks. I was asked if I would volunteer to serve as an instructor for the next eight weeks working with the next advanced training class. When I think back to that time, I really felt good about being called to be an instructor. After all, I was only eighteen years old. Upon finishing the second training cycle I was transferred to Fort Riley, Kansas and assigned to the 16th Infantry Regiment as a tanker. We were to participate in the U.S. Army's "Operation Gyro." This experiment would entail two full U.S. Army combat divisions to completely exchange their assignments with each other without moving any of their equipment. It was to be an awesome task.

The two divisions involved were the 10th Infantry Division, which was called the Mountain Division, and the 1st Infantry Division which was called the Big Red One Division. I was stationed in the Big Red One which was stationed at Fort Riley, Kansas, and we were going to exchange places with the Mountain Division which was stationed in Germany. Somewhere in the midst of this complicated experiment, it was determined that more Military police were needed to police all of the troop activities. I was asked to volunteer for Military Police training and was assigned to a provisional military police company. Even though I was somewhat apprehensive, very soon I realized that I had found my first love, LAW ENFORCEMENT.

The three years that I spent in the Army, and especially the two years I spent in Germany, were a watershed in my life. I went into the military service as a boy and came out a man. Even now as we live in the era of all voluntary military service I wonder what would have happened to me if I had not served a tour in the U.S. Army.

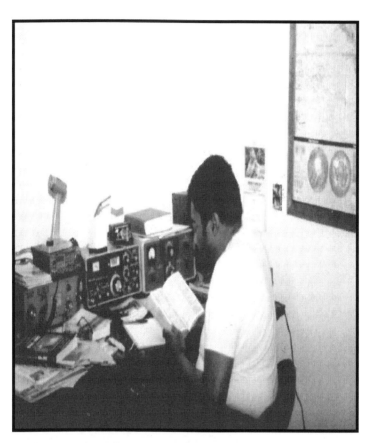

A new hobby – Morse Code!

10

FOREIGN AFFAIRS

Ultimately I decided I wanted to serve an Army tour in Germany. I wanted to see the world. I finally ended up in Germany in a place called Wildflecken. Back in those day (1956) most troops traveled to and from Germany via a big boat called a "Troop Ship". I was shipped to Fort Dix, New Jersey, then to New York City to board the ship USNS Upshur. I could still see the Statute of Liberty when my stomach began to turn over and it took only a minute before I was throwing up all over the place. A mixture of anxiousness and the movement of the ship was not a good recipe for me and it only got worse. When we got to England we stopped off in Southampton. Just about the time (we had been sailing for 6 days and I had sea legs) we pulled away from Southampton and into the North Sea, there arose one of those fierce storms which the North Sea is famous for. I do not wish to describe the suffering that I went through but I will say that I still have never been so glad to reach any place in my life as I was to reach Bremerhaven, Germany.

When I arrived in Germany I was assigned to the 373rd Armored Infantry Battalion and placed in a mortar platoon. We trained daily on learning how to fire the 81 millimeter mortar. The platoon consisted of a young 2nd Lieutenant, two or three sergeants, and two old soldiers, who were nothing but drunks. We thought that about the only thing they had going between them were all of those combat patches that they wore on the uniforms. These two guys were the truck drivers that supported us to and from the different firing ranges. I often wondered why the Army allowed the old drunks to stay enlisted.

One day we were out on the mortar firing range practicing. The mortar firing range consisted of a large hill where we set up mortars which fired a large 81mm missile. In the valley below this large hill, approximately three to four hundred yards away, was constructed three separate houses which were the target we were supposed to destroy. The lieutenant, since he was a college graduate, was acting as what we called a "Forward Observer." He would look through his binoculars and give us the range and the azimuth of the target. This information was needed so that you could accurately aim your mortar. The range was determined by raising or lowering the angle of your gun barrel. This was done by a crank mounted on the barrel. The azimuth told you how much to change the direction of your gun barrel from side to side. This information was determined by the portable sighting device that each gunner carried with him, and attached to the gun when he was firing.

The range that this type of weapon could fire was determined by the number of sacks of explosives you had attached to the base of the mortar shell. When you dropped the mortar shell into the gun base first, and it struck the base of the gun the explosives ignited, which propelled the shell forward. For example, if the shell contained five sacks of explosives, and the gunner felt you only needed three, he would yell "draw two," and the loader would snatch two of the sacks off of the shell. When he yelled "fire" you would drop the shell in the gun. I was the loader that day and we couldn't hit anything. We had three mortars set up on the hill and all three of us, responding to the commands of the 2nd Lieutenant, had been shooting at those three houses all morning. It seemed to me that the safest place to have been that morning was in those three houses.

When the lunch break came the two old drunks took great pleasure in razzing all of us "cruits", because we couldn't hit the targets. One of them said that he could hit all three targets at the same time without an aiming device. Finally, the 2nd Lieutenant got tired of them bragging and made them stand at attention, and for our benefit told the old soldiers that if they thought they were that good he wanted them to demonstrate for us. The old soldiers agreed. They walked over to one of the mortars, pulled the base plate that it was mounted on out of the ground, and reset it. They removed the aiming device saying that they would not need it. One of the old soldiers stood behind the mortar and looked across the barrel at the houses. He then barked some instructions to the other soldier. And after cranking the barrel up or down and side to side, he said "fire one". We sat still holding our breath while the missile was in the air. Finally it landed. And it missed the targets! We took great pleasure in laughing heartily. The old timer was again barking instructions and all I heard was "Fire for Effect". We watched with fascination as the second soldier dropped one round, made a few adjustments, dropped a second round, made a few additional adjustments and dropped the third round. As we sat puzzled, there was an explosion in the valley and the first house blew up. A few seconds later there was another explosion, and the second house blew up, and finally, the third house blew up. It was the most amazingly skilled display of gunmanship I have ever seen. It was later revealed that those two old army soldiers, both black, served in World War II and the

Korean Conflict in an old all black fighting regiment. Both served in a heavy weapons company and had been mortar men. Both were alcoholics and the U. S. Army was the only home and family they had. I now understood why the U.S. Army kept its old drunks in the army when possible. These two were men of legendary war achievements and were always willing to place their lives on the line for their country.

This all occurred in the winter of 1956. Later on, Europe experienced one of the coldest winters that it experienced in over fifty years. As a foot soldier I had to go out in the cold every day. When I was not in training, I was serving on guard duty. Finally the temperature dropped to thirty four below zero. It was so cold that normally when we stood guard duty we worked outside for two hours and then came in and rested for four hours. This schedule went on for a complete day, which meant that you worked for eight hours and was off for sixteen hours. When the temperature dropped to negative thirty-four degrees, we could only work outside for thirty minutes and come inside for one hour. I only had to do this once and I was ready to look for another job.

Remember all of those tests that I had to take when I first came into the Army? I gave those tests the best efforts that I had and the results came to my rescue again. One day after we came in from working in the cold all day, I was told to report to the Personnel Office at Battalion Headquarters. It seemed as though my battalion had a need for some Morse code trained radio operators. Since I scored high on the aptitude test I was asked if I was interested in attending the Radio Operator School in Darmstadt, Germany. My thought was simple. Would this get me out of the cold weather? The answer was yes and it proved to be my passport to an inside job. My radio squad had six radio operators and most of them were finishing up their tour of duty and going back to the states. Within six months of finishing radio school I was promoted to the position of Chief Radio Operator.

Shortly after I became the Chief Radio Operator we were able to get a new Morse code operator from the states. Imagine my surprise when I went to pick him up and found out he was a young black soldier from High Point, North Carolina. His name was Coyt L. Belo, and we hit it off immediately. Before long he and I pooled our money and purchased a 1951 car which allowed us to travel. On weekends when we were both off duty, we would drive up into the mountains to various places and drink beer with the young Germans. We really had a ball!

Before I leave this part of my army career, I want to tell you about another special person that God placed in my life that I owe a tremendous debt of gratitude. Shortly after I became the Chief Radio Operator, I got a new boss from stateside. He was a black 1st Lieutenant whose name was Homer Petite. He was a graduate from Prairie View College in Texas, which was the college that I planned to attend after I left the service. He was the first black commander that I worked for, so I thought that I could get away with a few things. Never was I so wrong. Because of my various "shenanigans" Lieutenant Petite finally called me in and demoted me. It was a big blow to my ego and I was crushed.

During his counseling session with me, the Lieutenant impressed upon me the fact that race had no place in being an effective manager. He then promoted one of my subordinates and placed him over me. Being childish, I asked for a transfer. Instead, he assigned me to a truck driving position. I quickly realized it was time to grow up. Lieutenant Petite taught me a lesson that not only would I not forget later in my law enforcement career, but it would serve me mightily in the coming years. I later found out through my friend Belo that Lieutenant Homer Petite retired from the Army as a General. I am sure it was well deserved because he taught me to take care of business, even if it required "TUFF" LOVE!

I completed my tour in Germany in late 1957 and due to the sickness I experienced coming over, I began to worry about what mode of transportation I would be assigned to on my return trip. Many of my friends were being flown back, however, I was not so fortunate. The only thing notably about my return trip was that on December 31st, while we were in the North Sea, midnight came and the ship celebrated the coming of the new year in a very grand way. It was now 1958, so what was the big deal? Well, approximately thirty minutes into the new year we entered a new time zone and we were back in 1957, which meant that later we had to celebrate the new year all over again!

After completing my military service in 1958, I returned to Houston and went to work. Later, I moved to Kansas City, Missouri and married my childhood sweetheart, Pearl Dietrich Bedford.

Me and the mother of my children, Pearl B. Swift

11

MY FIRST LOVE

I first met Pearl Bedford at the Saint John Baptist Church on Dowling Street in Houston, Texas. She was thirteen and I was fifteen. For me, it was either love at first sight or something darn close. Pearl sang in the church choir and even as a teenager she had an amazing voice. She was a striking young lady with quiet beauty, a radiant smile and the most commanding presence. She was tall, of medium size, had brownish-red skin tone and keen features. She had a warm and mature personality which drew most, young and old, into her presence. I think I paid more attention to her instead of the sermons the preacher preached. The way I use to tell the story to my children is that she chased me because I was the "catch" and all the young ladies wanted me. In my version of the story, after church service all the little teenage girls, including Pearl, would come up to me and bat their eyes and openly flirt, but she was the lucky one to catch my attention. She described events a little different. She said that I was a tall, lanky young man with perfect teeth and a captivating smile and that I made advances toward her every Sunday like clockwork. After my encounters with the ladies of the congregation, Pearl would whisk by me and walk outside. Now I must interject that she would brush up against me to get my attention, then once outside she would wait for me to follow her. She used to say she would reject me when I asked her out and that's what probably kept me coming back to her. She found joy in telling the children that I would walk on my eyebrows to be with her. You can imagine the pleasure our children took in hearing the varied versions about our courtship. In truth, I think that it was me that was more smitten, and not her.

Pearl's father passed away shortly before her graduation from Jack Yates High School, which was the cross town rival of my school, Phyllis Wheatley Senior High School. I used to have to sneak over to see her because the Jack Yates boys did not appreciate us coming into their territory to court their girls. After Pearl graduated from high school she moved to Kansas City, Missouri. While I was away in the Army, I missed her greatly and went to see her one time when I was stationed at Fort Riley, Kansas. When I left Houston and went to Germany we wrote each other from time to time but nothing serious seemed to develop from this. I guess you could say we were more or less "pen pals". When I got out of the army I immediately went to seriously court Pearl. She was the woman that I wanted to marry. She was the woman that I wanted to be the mother of my children. I even agreed to leave Houston and move to Kansas City, Missouri if she would marry me!

In June of 1958 Pearl and I were married at the Saint Stephen's Baptist church, located at Truman Road and Paseo. Matthew Bennett was the best man and Pearl's best friend, Wanda Nelson, was her maid of honor. Pearl and I went on to have five children and were married for nineteen years. We divorced in 1977. She was a wonderful person and I always attributed our breakup to my then inability to be a loving and nurturing husband.

12

SURVIVING THE EARLY DAYS

In August of 1958 I joined the Kansas City Missouri Police Department as a patrol officer, and after a rather rocky beginning, began my rapid ascent up through the ranks of the Kansas City Police Department. But first, before my road gets "rocky", I want to mention another one of my "heroes", one whose values and integrity has had a tremendous impact upon shaping me as a law enforcement officer, as well as the Christian man that I became.

Back in the fifties, it was the custom to have a black officer train any new black recruit. I was assigned to a young officer, Alvin Brooks. Now, that was not bad, but this young officer, who was four years older than me, was in disfavor on the police department. He had broken an unwritten rule - that you did not assist any blacks who had been the victim of the miscarriages of justice, which happened quite often during this period of time, throughout the United States.

A few things were working against him. (1) It had been brought to his attention that a young black male had been wrongfully convicted of a murder which Officer Brooks discovered he had not committed. When he attempted to get the police department to look further into this wrongful incarceration they refused. He then indicated that he would investigate it further on his own, and (2) Officer Brooks had requested permission to go to college. Regarding the first item the department held against him, Officer Brooks worked on the case of the young man who had been convicted, until he solved the case, and got the young man released from prison. Meanwhile many of the white officers considered him to be a traitor, and refused to speak to him.

The commanders of the police department were incensed. How dare this young "uppity" black attempt to see that justice was done, *and* he had the nerve to want to go to college. The department's response to this would be laughable today, but their response was not unusual for America in the 1950s.

Officer Brooks had been assigned to patrol the predominately black part of the city. In fact, his beat was 12th Street. Yes the famous intersection of 12th and Vine was a part of his beat. It also later turned out to be my first patrol assignment. The police department decided to change Officer Brooks' assignment and assigned him to patrol the bottom land along the Missouri River and the Choteau Bridge. There was nothing in that area except farm land and varmints. When I drew Officer Brooks as my Trainee Instructor, I found myself thinking I would never be able to learn anything out there in the boondocks.

As it turned out, since Officer Brooks had very little to do but train me, I don't think that any of the other recruits were trained as well as I was. I was very well equipped. One evening we were in the basement of a truck line and Officer Brooks was writing reports when he asked me how fast I could draw my pistol, to which I answered that I did not know. He told me that we learned how to shoot accurately in the academy, but not how to get our weapons out quickly. He then gave me a demonstration which I will never forget. He went outside and found a few small rocks, came back and emptied out his 38 caliber police revolver. He held his gun hand out before him and laid a small rock on the back of his hand. He told me to tell him when to draw and to make note of the difference between the time the rock struck the floor and the sound of his pistol clicking. When I said "fire", he was so quick to draw and fire that I was not able to tell which sound I heard first. He then had me replicate what he had done. Without embarrassing myself, I will only say that a significant time elapsed between the sound of my rock hitting the floor and my pistol going "click". Officer Brooks admonishment to me was that I was young, big and black and that he would guarantee me that upon completion of recruit training I would be assigned to the roughest black neighborhoods. And that is exactly what happened. In order to prepare me properly, for the next six weeks of my training, each day Officer Brooks would have me standing in that basement office for fifteen to thirty minutes practicing drawing my empty pistol and pulling the trigger. Even though I was never as fast as him, I must admit I got pretty "SWIFT". Alvin Brooks taught me to always be ready for whatever I was confronted with, he taught me readiness.

My second story involves a little restaurant down in the "bottoms" where Al and I would periodically stop in and get a bowl of chili to take out. One particular day we decided to eat inside of the restaurant. When we ordered, the waitress started to put the chili in a paper container. When we told her that we were going to eat it inside, the young waitress' face turned red and she told us, "We do not serve coloreds inside." Even though I was

67

quite angry, I could not help but laugh when Alvin responded by saying, "That's ok, we don't eat coloreds." A few weeks later we got a call back to the same restaurant on a bunch of young white males fighting inside. I happened to be the driver at that time and we were quite a bit away. I drove slowly as I was in no hurry to get there to defend this racist establishment. Alvin jumped my frame mightily and cut the red lights and siren on the patrol car to get us there in record time. Afterwards, he wanted to know why I was taking my time answering the call. I reminded him that those folk would not let us eat inside. He explained to me that I was obligated regardless of how I felt. Alvin Brooks taught me to allow my sense of obligation and duty to always guide my responses. Officer Brooks was truly one of the people who not only touched my life in a very special way, but also touched many others. He later left the department and finished his education, then came back to the City of Kansas City, Missouri as the Director of the Human Relations Department. I lost track of Alvin, but after serving his community as a Civil Rights leader he went into politics and was elected to the City Council, served as the Mayor Pro Tem and later was appointed to the Board of Police Commissioners of the department that he once served on.

Now, let me share with you my early wars with the Kansas City Missouri Police Department.

13

TROUBLED BEGINNINGS

My initial problem was that I was always in conflict with my superiors because they wanted to treat the white officers one way and the black officers a different and less equitable way. I was always fighting back, pointing out the difference in how blacks were treated and documenting acts of unequal treatment.

The trouble first began when I submitted a request to attend the local junior college. I was told by my superiors that I would not ever have use for college. I very respectfully disagreed. Finally, upon my insisting, I was granted my wish and placed on another shift under the supervision of a white supervisor who was noted for his dislike of blacks. He already had two black officers that were on his shift, and now he had a third. That was not a good situation. This patrol supervisor called all of the white officers under his supervision by their names, however, the two black officers he called "Midnight" and "Blacknight." One night he stopped by my patrol area to review some reports I had prepared. When he started to drive off he called me "Night Train," I STOPPED HIM IN HIS TRACKS and we exchanged a few unkind words. When he told me the other black patrolmen did not mind him calling them their nicknames, I told him that I would always address him by his rank and name and I expected him to give me the same respect. He drove off in a huff and my life became miserable from that point onward. In his eyes, I could never do anything right after that.

You can imagine the struggles that I had as a rookie. There were no black superiors we could turn to and even when I tried to get the few black officers to stand together, they were more concerned about keeping their jobs than they were about being treated equally. In 1961 I was brought upon several trumped up charges and advised to resign or be fired. In their minds, I had the audacity to insist that I have a hearing before the Board of Police Commissioners. I was entitled to this appeal, but instead I was brought up on charges before the Chief of Police. The Chief immediately recognized that I was being pushed out the door because of my demands for equal treatment, but for his success, he had to stand with his senior commanders. He suspended me for fourteen days without pay, which was a punishment that was not subject to appeal to the Board. He then recommended that I seek employment elsewhere because he knew that I would be hounded until I left the department.

I could write a book about all of the harassment that I went through at that time. I took the fourteen day suspension, went to Texas and told my father I would probably be coming back to him and to keep a truck driving job open. He assured me that he would. But the longer I was off, the madder I became. I was not going to let those people run me off of a job that I loved and was good at it. I decided to fight. I developed a survival strategy:

- I would work hard at being the best police officer that I could;
- I would not complain about anything, I would just take it;

- I would make sure that my personal life was above reproach, and
- I would study hard and take every examination I could.

That was in 1961. The end results were:

- I was promoted to Patrol Sergeant in 1967
- I was promoted to Patrol Lieutenant in 1969
- I was promoted to Captain, Director of Community Relations in 1969
- I was promoted to Major, Patrol Division Commander in 1974
- I was promoted to Lieutenant Colonel, Commander of Operations and later Assistant Chief of Police in 1976.

Not all of these promotions were easy. I was able to get promoted to the rank of Captain just by excelling in the department's promotional process. After the rank of Captain all promotions were appointments made by the Chief of Police. You then had to hold that rank in a temporary manner until you performed to the Chief's satisfaction for two years, then you were granted the rank permanently.

I received a great amount of resistance to the rank of Major and the former Police Chief, who was now the Director of the Federal Bureau of Investigations and the Mayor of Kansas City, Missouri, had to intervene. Efforts were made by several high ranking law enforcement officers to block my promotion to Lieutenant Colonel because they wanted one of their favorites to get this rare promotion. The Kansas City Police Department had a relatively new Chief at that time. Joseph McNamara PhD, had retired from the New York City Police Department and had been selected to head the Kansas City Department. He later went on to become the Chief of Police in San Jose, California. Dr. McNamara insisted upon my promotion to the rank of Lieutenant Colonel. He was an outstanding Chief and he and I worked feverishly to eliminate police officers firing at fleeing unarmed criminals when they posed no threat to either the officer or the public. I continued that fight as long as I was in law enforcement. I retired from the Kansas City Missouri Police Department in 1985, having served more than twenty-seven years, the last nine in a senior management position.

I must mention another giant of a person that God placed in my life. He was Clarence M. Kelley, who was the Chief of Police of the Kansas City Department before he went back to Washington D.C. as the Director of the Federal Bureau of Investigation (FBI). In August of 1961 Clarence Kelley retired from the FBI and was selected as the Police Chief of Kansas City. I had recently been eliminated from the police department's Sergeant's promotion list and I did what you would have expected me to do. I submitted to the new Chief a formal memorandum asking that he look into how blacks were treated in the department. Not only did he respond to my complaint personally, he asked me to convene a number of black officers to meet with him.

At that time there were many positions in the department that blacks could not be assigned to. Positions such as:

- Detectives
- Inspectors
- Supervisors
- Motorcycle Officers
- Canine Officers, and
- Warrant Service Officers

There were other positions that we never occupied also, such as Polygraphists. When we began our meeting Chief Kelley brought in several of his top ranking officers to hear our complaints. At some point the Chief stood up with great indignation and walked out of the room after telling the high Brass that he wanted this problem solved immediately and that if he ever got such a complaint again he was going to take a strong look at his commanders. We never saw so much shuffling, reassignments and promotions as we did after that meeting. The list that I had been kicked off of was canceled and a personnel evaluation company was hired out of Chicago, Illinois to come in and study our department. Their recommendations were then implemented as soon as practicable. One of those recommendations concerned the department's promotional system. When the new promotional examinations were given, I was one of the first to be promoted. The past practices that had prevailed for so long were discriminatory. I had already experienced and knew that in life people will always try to knock you down. But I learned early on that as long as you get back up, you're showing them that you will stand up for what you believe in, even if you stand alone.

A few months later I was instrumental in stopping a potential riot between a large crowd of blacks and our police, in Kansas City, Missouri's Swope Park. As a result, I was featured on the news that evening by one of the national news TV programs. (I believe it was ABC News). Chief Kelley, who was present at the site of the disturbance, then sent for me and assigned me to work out of his office as the Director of Community Relations. Clarence Kelley became like a father figure and his management style served as an excellent example for me. Years later, after he retired from being the FBI Director and moved back to Kansas City, I wrote him a letter and told him that I did not want either of us to leave this earth before he knew what a giant influence he had on my life. Clarence M. Kelley, another one of my "heroes".

After that, my promotions began to come fairly rapidly. By the age of thirty-nine I became the youngest Lieutenant Colonel in the history of the Kansas City Missouri Police Department. I'm humbled by all of these experiences and I share them with you proudly because I know these successes were not of my own initiative. I may not have realized it at that time, however, I do now.

Religion and my Police career

During the twenty seven years that I spent at the Kansas City Missouri Police Department, my attendance and involvement in any kind of religious activity consisted of an occasional visit to a church once in a while for a special event, and a couple of years of membership in my first wife's congregation of Jehovah's Witnesses, back in 1970. I quickly learned that the Jehovah Witness doctrinal teaching did not square with what I had been taught in the Baptist church and their teachings on many subjects were incomprehensible to me. I quickly left the congregation, however, one way or another I still attended a church from time-to-time. Because I had been raised up in the Baptist church I thought that going to church occasionally was a nice thing and the right thing to do.

Colonel Leroy V. Swift

14

THE HOLY SPIRIT FOUND ME

By 1985 I was very happy with my assignment and only needed three to four more years before I could retire on a full pension. I had a very nice suite of offices on the command floor of the police department, overlooking downtown Kansas City. I was well known throughout the community and state as a very effective police administrator and had gained a nation-wide reputation within the law enforcement community in the field of Police Community Relations. And, I was earning more money than I ever could have dreamed of and thought I really had it made.

On the national scene, I had been instrumental in founding two national police organizations. One such organization was the "National Association of Police Community Relations Officers" (NAPCRO), which had been founded by a group of Police Community Officers gathered in Saint Louis, Missouri, to develop new strategies to enhance the interaction of our police departments with our communities. We recognized the need to interact with each other and exchange ideas on a regular basis. Thus, we founded NAPCRO. Additionally, in 1976, the U. S. Justice Department hosted a group of thirty high ranking black officers from throughout the United States. We gathered for a three day symposium in Silver Springs, Maryland to discuss problems that were problematic in our communities and explored ways that our senior black police executives could use their unique skills to reduce or eliminate some of the problems in our communities. One of the first problems that concerned us was that we did not know one another. Our solution to that problem was to establish an on-going forum to assist us in communicating with one another. Thus, the "National Organization of Black Law Enforcement Executives" (NOBLE), was formed. Today NOBLE continues to grow and strengthen its stature as an organization that has become a preeminent law enforcement association and provides resources for the law enforcers and the community.

During this period I very seldom thought about my life as a kid growing up in the backwoods of Texas, and even less did I think about getting my spiritual house in order. I encountered the possibility of death on more than one occasion during my law enforcement career and considered myself to be very lucky to come through all of those challenging situations and remain unscarred, both physically and mentally. That was my reality on that fateful day when I came face-to-face with the Holy Spirit!

It was a Monday morning in January of 1985 and I was standing at the window behind my desk gazing across the downtown Kansas City, Missouri City Hall lawn watching a building under construction. I was at peace with the world and was just giving some thoughts to a presentation I was preparing to make to the Police Executive Committee. I was a long time member of this committee which was responsible for managing the affairs of our department. I do not recall what the topic of the presentation was but since I was the Director of Administration for the Police Department, I was accustomed to making presentations of this sort. All of a sudden there occurred what appeared to be an explosion inside of me, and I heard this loud voice saying "IT IS TIME!" I was so frightened that I fell back into my chair and sat there, stunned. Finally, I said in a small voice, "Yes Lord". You see, I knew that the Holy Spirit was talking to me. I even had a "knowing" about what was meant by the words "IT IS TIME". Finally, still in a daze, I began to flip the pages of my desk calendar and my eyes came to rest on the date, March 22, 1985, which happened to be my daughter Cheryl's twenty-sixth birthday. Without knowing why, at that moment I wrote the following initials across the page "LWD", then picked up the phone to call Karen, my second wife, at her school.

Karen was a highly accomplished person and had risen to become one of, if not the first, female principal of a Senior High School in the Kansas City Public School system. When I got her on the phone I asked her to go to her office so she could see her desk calendar. She became uneasy and wanted to know if I was ok. I said yes, but she sensed that something was different with me. When she reached her office I asked her to write "LWD" on her desk calendar on March 22, 1985. She asked me why and I told her what those letters "LWD" meant, because now I understood. They meant that March 22nd was to be my "Last Work Day" on the Kansas City, Missouri Police Department.

I told Karen that I had been visited that morning by the Holy Spirit and I had to retire from the Kansas City, Missouri Police on March 22nd and go back to the "backwoods" of Central Texas where I was from to join the church of my childhood, the Mount Tabor Baptist Church. Of course Karen concluded that I was losing my mind and invited me to go see the police psychologist. I understood her reaction because this whole experience left me with a very eerie feeling that I could not explain. All that I really knew was that another "season" in my life was coming to a close and I had to move on.

I then went in to see the Chief of Police to advise him of what happened to me and to let him know that he needed to start looking for a Police Commander to elevate to my position. He looked at me with strange blank eyes and told me that he would wait awhile to allow me to "re-think" my decision. I don't think anyone that close to retirement, in such a high position, had ever just simply upped and retired. Later, after I had reaffirmed my decision to retire, the Chief, who was a long time friend of mine and used to work for me, told me that a new high ranking civilian position would be opening up shortly on the Police Department. He said that since it was under the Board of Police Commissioners, he would ask if they would hold this position for me for six months, in case I wanted to come back.

I found myself thinking about how nice it was to have good friends in high places. Nevertheless, I knew that something inside of me had changed. I knew at that very moment, even though I had not considered myself to be a "real" Christian, my mind was made up and come what may, I was going to serve the Lord....Jehovah God for the rest of my life. It was not until sometime later in my life that I realized that I had been responding to the call that God had placed on my life. I only knew that I now was willing to forsake everything in my life to serve God!

One day as I was studying the Word of God in the Book of Matthew I ran across a place where Jesus was teaching his followers about serving God.

*"And everyone that hath forsaken houses, or
brethren, or sisters, or father, or mother, or wife,
or children, or lands, for My name's sake, shall
receive an hundredfold, and shall inherit
everlasting life."* [Matthew 19:29 KJV]

My preparing to leave the Kansas City Missouri Police Department at the pinnacle of my career turned out to be a very amusing time for me. I saw the many puzzled looks by my co-workers. One of my subordinates who had hardly ever visited my office without an invitation began to drop by each day and inquire as to how I was feeling. He did it in a joking manner but I knew that he was serious. I finally called a staff meeting of my command staff to clear this matter up once and for all. But when I tried to explain why I was leaving the department early - THAT THE LORD HAD CALLED ME - many of them just went away shaking their heads. They knew that I had not been the religious type, so I am sure they thought that I had "lost it".

I think back to that time of my life, and even though I know so much more about walking in God's divine will now, which was not the case then, I knew that I wanted to heed God's call on my life. After all, he had simply said for me to give up my life of luxury and go back home where I had nothing and owned nothing except a 1/9th of 1/11th interest in the family's undivided estate from my grandfather, August "Gus" Long.

On March 22, 1985 I retired from the Kansas City Police Department without much fanfare. Oh, the local news media had a field day and I received many accolades according me the honor of being a black pioneer in the field of law enforcement management. But, other than that, I was able to slip quietly away. All of my children honored me by coming down to police headquarters to my office and escorting me home. That too, was one of the great moments in my life. Another great moment in my life relative to law enforcement was the day my youngest son, Joe, finished the Police Academy in DeKalb County in Georgia. Oh such pride that went through me as my son followed my footsteps.

Seven days later I loaded some things into my old pickup truck that I purchased for use in the country, and headed for Texas. I was forty-eight years old, retired, and had no idea what the future held for me. The only thing that I was sure about was that I wanted to serve the Lord, however He wanted me to serve Him.

When I arrived in Texas I moved into the family's old mobile home with my baby brother Bennie. He was just a little kid when I left home for military service so I really did not know much about him and I was looking forward to being able to establish a brotherly relationship with him. That was one of the few pluses that I saw in my new circumstances. I brought some of my amateur radio equipment with me, since that was my favorite hobby. I have been a licensed Amateur Operator since 1958 and I have held an "Amateur Extra Class license with the call sign of KN0Y since 1981. I was also very active in a military program called the "Navy Military Affiliate Radio System" or Navy MARS. I quickly set up a radio station and started to do some radio-teletype work transferring messages around the United States from military personnel overseas. This kind of radio work dates back to my Morse code days in the U.S. Army.

The first Sunday that I was back in Gause was Easter Sunday of 1985 and I went to Mount Tabor Baptist Church for the first time in many years, without there being a family funeral. On Easter Sunday I dressed in a nervous silent state, not knowing what would be expected of me. I drove over to the church and what I saw remains vivid in my memory, even today. There was this old, raggedy, or maybe I should say dilapidated church building sitting on two acres of tall weeds. When I went inside I saw two or three women and no men. As I sat there wondering what I was doing, one of the ladies, whom I did not know (the other one had been brought in from an area nursing home) approached me and asked if I would help her "open up" the church. I had no clue as to what she meant, since the doors had been opened when I arrived. So I politely told her that I would be unable to do so.

Later, the Pastor stood in the pulpit and preached. I got no meaning out of his sermon, but, was I supposed to? I did not know. I did know that this church needed help and that God sent me back home to be its helper. When the invitation was extended, much to everyone's surprise, I got up and went forward. I told the few assembled that the Holy Spirit had sent me back home and that I had no idea what to do, but I would be doing whatever was necessary from that time on. I told them that when the building was opened I would be the one opening it. When the grass needed cutting I would be the one doing it. I told them that whatever needed to be done either I would do it or find someone who could. I am proud of the fact that for the next fifteen years I can count on one hand the number of times I missed church services at Mount Tabor Baptist. I mowed that two acre lawn for the next seventeen years and taught a Sunday School class for the next fifteen years and still managed to serve as the deacon, the church clerk and the church musician. Now my odyssey, my walk "to" Christ, was becoming a walk "with" Him. How fulfilling my life was becoming.

Following that Easter Sunday service I interviewed Mount Tabor's Pastor, who was married to one of my aunts, and asked him what I needed to do to open up the doors of the church. He told me that I needed to come in front of the church congregation, read a scripture and kneel before the congregation and give a prayer. I almost went into shock. I could certainly read a scripture but I had never prayed in my life, except for the prayer that my mama taught us when we were little kids....I still remember that prayer:

"As I lay me down to sleep
I pray to the Lord my soul to keep
If I should die before I wake
I pray the Lord my soul to take."

There was no question in my mind now that my walk with Christ had started. I went before the Lord the only way I knew and I thanked Him for bringing me safely through all of life's dangerous highways and byways. You see, my spiritual eyes had finally begun to open and I realized where all of my "luck" had come from. I told the Lord that I wanted to be HIS servant and I wanted to serve HIM all of my remaining life. I asked Him to put a prayer in my mouth and give me the courage to go before that small congregation and pray.

Isn't that something? This big (two hundred and fifty pounds) veteran police officer, who made thousands of arrests of all kinds of violent and dangerous individuals and had spoken before thousands in his capacity as a law enforcement leader during his career, was afraid to stand before my little church congregation and pray out loud. But, God is good!

During the week I was able to borrow a small push lawnmower and after several days work I had the church grounds looking acceptable. As I pushed the lawnmower in the hot Texas sun with the sweat dripping from my face, at some point I noticed I had tears streaming down my cheeks and I wondered why. After all, I was not the emotional type, I thought. I didn't believe that it was "manly" to cry, yet the tears were real and continued, inexplicably, to fall. Finally I stopped in my tracks and confronted myself. It was at that time that I realized I was crying tears of joy. What a dramatic change had occurred in my life. In a relatively short time I had gone from being the Assistant Chief of Police of a major city, to being a "yard boy" in a little country church in the backwoods of Texas. I realized then that I HAD NOT FOUND GOD, HE FOUND ME! My search for the Lord was over. All I had to do now was walk in obedience before Him. This experience was one of life's precious moments. That experience, and those tears of joy, remains one of the highlights of this odyssey. But I still had a long way to go.

The following Sunday I went before the congregation and read a scriptural passage. I then got down on my knees and prayed aloud before the congregation.

15

NEW BEGINNINGS

At some point I noted that Mount Tabor Baptist Church did not have a Sunday School so I asked if I could start teaching a class to whomever showed up and the church was glad to give me that responsibility. Now I had a problem, I did not know anything about the Bible or teaching God's Word. Oh, I had taught in law enforcement circles and had spoken at workshops and seminars across the country, but teach God's Word - now that was a different proposition.

I prayed to Jehovah God and petitioned Him to empower me to teach His Word. I asked God for His special anointing upon my life so that I could teach His Word **and** teach it His ways. God granted me this request and I came to love teaching the Word of God. Very soon I was often invited by other area churches to be a lay teacher or speaker for them at special functions. I praise the Lord that He gifted me to teach back then and He has continued to bless me to do so.

Lord - I need a Help mate!

My wife from Kansas City divorced me because I refused to return to Kansas City, in spite of a lucrative job offer. She seriously felt that I had lost my mind. She tried to comfort me, to rationalize with me, to help me to understand that my thinking was skewed. But my thinking and my heart were both crystal clear. I knew that Kansas City served its season in my life and that season was over. My wife was not a country girl, and I was a country boy so I didn't fully expect her to join me. My feet became firmly planted, not in Texas, but in my walk toward Christ and I didn't want anything or anyone to jeopardize that. I understood that we were at odds and I didn't blame her for wanting a divorce.

Finally I felt the need to get a job. After all, I was only forty eight years old. I began applying for several Chief of Police jobs in Texas and one finally began to look very promising, even to the point that I was quite sure I would get it. For me this posed a dilemma, the city was over two hundred miles from my church. I again sought God in prayer and reminded Him that I promised that when the doors of Mount Tabor Baptist opened, I would open them, and whatever needed to be done in the church, I would do. I prayed to the Lord that it looked like I was about to be appointed to this Chief's job which was far away, and it would be hard for me to carry out my promises to Him. Guess what? I did not hear from that city again for a very long time.

A few weeks later I was walking up and down the dirt road in front of my brother's house barefooted, enjoying the warm sand flowing between my toes. That is something I used to love to do as a kid. While I was walking I stopped at the mailbox. In it was a letter asking me if I was interested in coming to work for the City of Austin, Texas. Imagine that. I had not applied for any jobs in

Austin, so the invitation seemed strange. I figured this must have been a mistake because the letter was from the City's Parks and Recreation Department's personnel officer. I found myself thinking, "I" am a law enforcement officer, I don't know anything about parks. The personnel officer even had his home phone number on the letter. I could tell that he was serious, but felt he just made a mistake and sent the letter to the wrong person. I asked myself, how did he get my address? Then I remembered that the Chief of Police in Austin, Texas was an old friend of mine. He and I graduated from the Southern Police Institute at the University of Louisville, Kentucky back in 1970.

When I called I was advised that the City of Austin, Texas had a vacant position for a Chief of Police for the Austin Park Police. Was I interested? Would I come in for an interview? I immediately saw the hand of God in all of this. After all, Austin was only seventy five miles from my church and I could very easily drive there on Sundays.

In a short period of time, I was appointed to the position of Chief of the City of Austin's Park Police and I held that position for eleven years, retiring for the second time at the age of sixty. Here again, is another example of how Jehovah God's Holy Spirit has worked in my life and taken care of me in ways that for me were inexplicable. The salary for Austin's Park Police Chief's position was slightly less than the one for the other Chief's job, but was most adequate for my needs. However, a very interesting thing occurred concerning my salary at the Austin Park Police. After I had been working there for approximately two months, my superiors called me in and give me a substantial raise, elevating my salary to above what I would have been making in the other Police Chief position. I was awestricken. Their excuse for giving me the unsolicited raise was that they wanted my salary to be more comparable to what I had been making in Kansas City. *Nope*, I thought, Jehovah God was rewarding me for my faithfulness! You see, I had been in the process of buying a home in Austin but had been turned down because my income was not enough to qualify for the mortgage loan that I needed. I now was able to qualify for the loan and purchased the house.

Another interesting thing occurred during this time. The day after I went to work for the City of Austin I received a letter from the city that previously stopped corresponding with me, asking me to come in for final interviews for the Chief's position. I saw evidence of God's hand all around me. It was simply beyond my comprehension, the things that were going on in my life. The odyssey continued.

After my divorce I was very lonely and craved a companion to share my walk with Christ. I knew she had to be a God fearing woman. I prayed often for God to send me such a companion. In the meantime I was determined to walk uprightly before my God in obedience. In 1986 God answered my prayers and sent me a God-fearing woman to be my mate. Her name was Marjorie Hill Williams and she was an elementary school teacher. She was my pride and joy and I just enjoyed being with her. But, very early in our marriage she was diagnosed with a blood disorder which her doctor said would eventually lead to leukemia and that it would be terminal. When I asked the doctor how long we should expect before her health deteriorated, he indicated two to three years, and we both were devastated.

My wife was a much stronger Christian than I was and simply did not believe that she was going to die in the next couple of years. How I glorified in her faith. My daily prayer to God was that

He allow her to walk by my side in accordance with His will. That walk lasted thirteen years!

For fifteen plus years I worked faithfully at the Mount Tabor Baptist Church. I was able to get the building fixed, I kept the yard mowed (I now had a riding lawn mower) and, as I indicated earlier, I became the Church's Deacon, clerk, Sunday school teacher, as well as the janitor and "Jack of all trades."

I was doing just fine as the church's janitor until early one Sunday morning I arrived to clean up the building before church services. When I came to the console piano I lifted the top and peeked in and noticed a large pile of debris. I assumed the mice had been nesting in the piano, so I decided to just clean all of the debris out. I could not see clearly into the piano but I reached my hand inside and grabbed the nest, and it started to wiggle. When I was finally able to look into my hand, I was holding a big old snake! I still smile when I remember taking "one giant leap backward for mankind!" I had always been afraid of snakes. So I dropped him back into the piano and fled the church. As I was running I knew that we couldn't have church worship services that day, not with a snake in it. I thought, *it's either me or the snake, and the snake won*. I finally calmed down, came to my senses and decided that if there was ever a time that I needed to pray, it was then. God never fails us. I was able to find a man over in the Gause Township who kept snakes as pets. I went and picked him up and he came down and captured the snake and carried him away. My faith was tested that day and God taught me a lesson that He was in charge and nothing stood in the way of fulfilling his purpose. We had church!

Slowly Mount Tabor began to grow until finally it had a congregation of approximately twenty members. I was able then to divest myself of some of my responsibilities and take longer vacations. In 1996 after I retired from the City of Austin, my wife said that she wanted to travel and see Europe before she went home to be with the Lord. I wanted so badly to give her as much as I could, she deserved so much more. We traveled throughout eight different countries in Europe, and had ourselves a ball.

In 1995 I built a home for us to retire on my farm, which was adjacent to Mount Tabor Baptist Church. Since I was retired, I was still the one who went down early on the cold Sunday mornings and lit the heaters and kept the grounds up. But most of the administrative and secretarial work was passed on to the younger members in the church. What a relief. The odyssey continued.

My Wife went home to Glory

In 1999 I lost my wife to Leukemia but the Holy Spirit, the Comforter, sustained me during that period. I was scheduled to be the keynote speaker at a banquet the day after my wife's funeral. Everybody thought that I should cancel the speaking engagement, but I thought that it would keep my mind busy, and that is what happened. I think it ended up being one of my most inspiring speeches, at least it was for me.

My retirement home in the country, which now belongs to my
daughter Renee.

16

MY MUSIC MINISTRY

I played music in high school and quit playing after I graduated and had gotten rid of my instrument. Since they had no musician I started back playing for Mount Tabor in 1989. As a Christian saxophonist I was asked also to play engagements outside of my church maybe once or twice each month. During the period right after my wife passed, the demands for my music seemed to explode. I was doing six to eight outside engagements each month. It was a while before I realized what was happening in my life. The Lord was keeping me busy. During this period it became very clear to me that the Lord called me to be a Christian teacher, as well as a musician and I thoroughly enjoy ministering in this fashion. I was sure my music ministry was going to fulfill my life until I was called home to be with Jesus. Well . . . maybe.

Since music has been a major part of the Swift family's heritage and an important part of my life, I would be remiss if I did not provide you with a little history and summary of my musical endeavors. As I indicated earlier, in December of 1949 the family of Leroy Swift, Sr. moved from Gause, Texas to Houston, Texas. The major purpose of this move was for me and my siblings to get a better education than was afforded them at the little two room country school which the Swift children attended in the Two-Mile community of Gause, Texas. Immediately the four oldest Swift children professed an interest in learning to play a musical instrument. My dad had been a very popular guitarist, piano player and Blues & Folk singer in the late 1920s and early 1930s throughout the Texas Brazos Valley and Little River Valley region in Central Texas. So this was no surprise. Daddy's musical career was cut short because of a tragic incident which occurred during his prime. In fact, the story that we children were told suggested that our father's musical career was cut short because he imbibed a bad batch of moonshine whiskey (which incidentally he had brewed) and it damaged his vocal cords. As a consequence, his kids never heard him sing. Even while speaking, Daddy's voice remained barely a whisper throughout the remainder of his life. My mother told us that the doctor told my father that he could correct this problem with a minor surgical procedure and Daddy agreed to allow the doctor to do so. The story goes that while Daddy was sitting in the doctor's office he heard a patient screaming with pain. My daddy literally ran out of the doctor's office and escaped, never to return. Maybe "like father – like son!" All of that notwithstanding, I remember Daddy playing the piano at our grandparents home in Gause. Looking back, I guess I would have to categorize him as a mean ragtime pianist.

Juanita Long Swift, our mother was also an excellent singer and sung in the various churches throughout the Gause, Texas area. So the music was just in the "Swift kids" blood. The baby girl, the 9th Swift kid, also went on to become an excellent Christian vocalist, organist and singer.

I was the oldest of the nine Swift kids, and the family decided that they would purchase my instrument first (they later purchased clarinets for my two oldest sisters and a trombone for my next brother). I was excited that I was going to be a musician, just like my daddy. However, I was not really sure what instrument I wanted to play. We could not afford a piano, and that was my first love. When my daddy and mother took me down to the Parker Music Company in Houston, Texas, I kind of drooled over the saxophones. They seem to be so complicated. Finally my mother told me that I had to make my choice and I chose an Alto Saxophone. I started to take elementary band classes at the E. O. Smith Junior High School in Houston and immediately started having problems mastering my instrument. But I kept after it until I was able to play with the rest of the kids.

After I graduated from E. O. Smith and transferred to the Phyllis Wheatley Senior High School, I continued to play the alto saxophone in the marching band but was relegated to the third chair (the chair in which the student with the lowest level of proficiency sat). Nonetheless, at last I was playing and marching in the great Phyllis Wheatley Wildcat Marching Band. What a departure from the little two room country school I attended in Gause. It was in my second year at Phyllis Wheatley that I joined the Saint John Baptist Church on Dowling Street in Houston and was allowed to join one of the church's two bands. It had both a senior band, which played only during the worship services, and a junior band which played for the Sunday School, as well as the worship services. Both of the bands marched in various community parades.

It was in that band that I met two young male band members that became like brothers to me, Marcellus Sykes and his younger brother, Alvin Sykes. Their mother, Luella Sykes became my second mother. Marcellus played the bass horn and Alvin was the drummer. The two of them even joined the four Swift kids and came down and played a special music concert overlooking the Little River Bottoms. I remember it like it was yesterday. I had only been playing my saxophone in the Saint John junior band for approximately two months when the Band Director, Brother Chapman, called me into his office and told me that he was taking my saxophone assignment away from me because I was not very good at it. Instead he decided to train me as a baritone horn player. He said it had more music written for it and he felt that I would make a better baritone player than a saxophonist.

I was somewhat sadden by the fact that it seemed as though my career as a saxophone player in the church band was over, but happy that I was able to continue playing the saxophone in the Phyllis Wheatley Marching Band. Brother Chapman immediately began training me as a baritone horn player, and I took to the instrument like, as my late mother would say, "a duck to water". I truly enjoyed the baritone horn. My confidence grew immensely and I walked and strutted and played my baritone in every parade my church marched in. I can still hear the march 'O When the Saints, Come Marching In" ringing in my ears when we paraded through the streets of Houston, with me and my baritone horn romping and stomping.

In the meantime, back at the high school I was still playing alto saxophone. I somewhat lost interest in it since it did not hold for me the excitement that I found in playing the baritone horn. But one day, as I sat in my third alto saxophone chair, the band was preparing to play in a concert and the band director was having difficulty getting the band to master a rather complicated orchestra selection. None of the three baritone horn players were able to play the difficult baritone horn solo, which was the key to a rather beautiful and moving passage. I borrowed the baritone music sheet and carried it home for the weekend. On the following Monday I sat quietly in my third chair in the alto saxophone section and listened as the baritone horn players continued to assassinate the beautiful passage. Professor Harris, our Band Director, was becoming quite frustrated. Rather shyly I raised my hand and asked the band director if I could try to play the piece on the baritone horn. My band director scoffed mightily at the thought and the band class cracked up with laughter. I thought the band director was going to join them in their laughter. After all, here was a third chair saxophonist, whose musical passages were simple at best, offering to play a very difficult musical passage that all of the seasoned baritonists had not been able to master. *Obviously he had no understanding of my playing the baritone horn player for my church*, I thought. He ignored my request.

For the rest of the day he continued to impress upon the three school baritone horn players the importance of mastering that selection. But I wanted to play that piece and needed to figure out a plan. I again raised my hand and requested to play the piece. Looking back in retrospect, I think that my band director was actually desperate and at that point willing to try anything. He invited me to borrow the third chair baritone's instrument and give it a try. What ensued was, and still remains one of the highlights of my young life. I devoured that piece. Of course, no one in the class realized that I had become quite an accomplished baritonist in my church's band. I now know that my desire to master that musical passage on the baritone was providential. The baritone horn and I performed magnificently. When I finished playing the piece, the silence was deafening. The band director then had me play a couple of additional pieces with the band and upon completion proudly announced to the remainder of the band that I was now the first chair baritonist. He told me to put up my saxophone because I would not need it again. Sadly, at the rather tender age of 16, my career as a saxophonist was over. I don't even recall what ultimately happened to my saxophone. I didn't care because I thought I would never play the saxophone again.

Let's fast forward approximately thirty two years to the year of 1985. I had given up playing the saxophone in 1953 and left music altogether when I finished Phyllis Wheatley High School in 1955. I finally bought a piano in 1983 quickly realized that my interest in it had also vanished.

Called to Play Christian – Again

One day while prowling the City of Austin I was drawn to a pawn shop, although I am not the pawn shopper type. As I was browsing the pawn shop I noticed an old beat-up alto saxophone with a cost of less than two hundred dollars. In spite of my lack of interest, I continued to return to that instrument. Since I did not have any money in my possession, I asked the pawn shop staff to place this instrument into their lay-a-way, which is something else I had never done in my life. At least I felt that I would recover from the temporary loss of sanity and asked the pawn shop employee if I changed my mind could I get my deposit back. I was assured that I could.

I went home and pondered over this rather inexplicable desire to purchase an alto saxophone. Somehow I knew it was "my" horn. I could not wait to purchase the saxophone so I went back to the pawn shop the following week and purchased the saxophone and brought it home. Now, I had a dilemma - what to do with this horn.

I had not played one, to any degree, for over thirty years and I certainly was not very good at it. *What to do, what to do?* I decided I would relearn to play the saxophone. The only piece of music I could find in my home was my Baptist hymn book. As I began to thumb through my hymn book I hoped to find a song I could use to begin practicing with. I finally called my sister Marian in San Antonio who was a professional Christian musician and I shared with her my dilemma. She went through her music and selected two songs for me to practice on. They were "Because He Lives" and "How Great Thou Art." So, every day I would take the old saxophone out when I got home and practice those two songs. My sister helped me tremendously by recording the piano music and sending it to me. She then taught me how to practice my songs with the piano music.

As my confidence grew I began to enjoy playing both pieces. I decided that if my church, Mount Tabor Baptist, would permit, I would like to bring my horn to church and play these two hymns for the congregation. The church had an old piano, but no musician. Since it was one of the old "backwoods" Baptist churches and several of the members were very elderly and did not take kindly to any kind of change in their worship service, I thought I should seek their permission before I tried to play for them. You can imagine my sense of intrepidness when I approached the old Deacon and told him what I proposed to do. He thought about it for a moment and finally agreed.

I really wanted to make a good impression on my church congregation. I called my sister again and asked if she and I could practice together, and if she would be willing to come to Mount Tabor to accompany me on the piano for the special church program that was being held. Marian graciously agreed and drove, on a few occasions, over to Austin from San Antonio to practice with me. These practice sessions ended up being a little rough because my baby sister had very high musical expectations of me and I probably did not meet up to her standards. However, she worked with me and lovingly fussed at me until she decided that my performance would at least be presentable. She then agreed to come to Mount Tabor and accompany me in my first musical presentation.

My first Christian musical performance at Mount Tabor is still another one of the milestones of my life. Here I stood as a musical soloist before the seventy to eighty people who had gathered for this special event. I began to feel excited and anxious and I, for one, thought I had simply lost my mind. The program proceeded smoothly and when it was my turn to render my musical selections, all of my mistakes were covered by Marian. Her brilliant piano playing made me sound like a real musician. I know today that without her encouragement and support, this aspect of my Christian Ministry would have never been a reality. With all of the bossing, fussing and her sense of perfection, she gave me the confidence to perform.

After the service was over the old deacon came to me and said, "Son, when you come back bring your horn." After listening to all of the comments from the "old folks" that day, I then knew in my spirit I had discovered another aspect to the "calling" that Jehovah God had placed in my walk. Several men and women of God had already prophesied over me that the Lord had a special calling on my life. I felt for the first time that I knew what it was, so my Christian Music Ministry was born.

Early Developments in my Music Ministry

After my first performance I realized I needed to find more music to play. My sister showed me how to transpose music from my hymn book into the proper key for the alto saxophone. As other churches became familiar with the Christian music that I played, I began to receive a steady flow of invitations to come and play for special church services, special events such as weddings, funerals, anniversaries, as well as other community activities. I was often amazed at the tremendous reception that my musical performances continued to receive. In spite of the fact that I had not been able to acquire an accompanist to go with me all the time to "make me sound beautiful", I continued to play. Finally, my sister suggested that I consider the use of pocket tapes. Pocket tapes, I asked, "What are those?" I began searching all of the Christian book stores in Austin trying to find accompaniment tapes with the music I liked to play. I developed quite a collection of old and new songs I could use for any kind of event. I also purchased a nice portable sound system I could haul around in my truck. I particularly liked the fact that I was now a "one man band", and did not need the additional help.

My preference was the old Christian favorites I enjoyed listening to such as "The Old Rugged Cross", which I used to love to hear my mama sing, and others such as "At the Cross", "How Great Thou Art", "Because He Lives", "His Eye is On the Sparrow", and "Glory to His Name". I also loved other songs I used to hear my mother sing, "I Surrender All", "In the Garden", and "I Must Tell Jesus". I bought a cassette carrier which held sixty tapes and soon filled it to capacity. I started to collect additional tapes as I traveled about the country. When I grew my collection to approximately ninety tapes, I decided to stop purchasing and just develop a list of selections from what I had. I began to pick out my favorites and transpose the music for my alto saxophone. Later, I purchased a tenor saxophone and transposed music for it also. I very seldom play the tenor because I truly consider myself to be an "alto saxophonist".

The invitations to play kept coming in. I finally realized that I could not handle all of the requests and I needed to become more selective. The Lord placed it on my heart that my music ministry was primarily for the "backwoods" areas where the churches had limited resources. Since this was my ministry, I never charged anything when I played. The Lord has blessed me so richly and I was humbled by the requests. I also believe in the invitation of Isaiah 55 where it says to come, all who are thirsty, come to the waters and you who have no money, come, buy, eat. Yes, this was my Christian Ministry and I was sharing spiritual food. I also felt a very special desire and responsibility to play for our senior citizens and nursing homes. I also wanted to bring Christian music to the prisons. So as to not over extend myself, I decided that outside of my church I would only play one musical engagement each month. Well, the idea of playing one outside engagement was the first artificial constraint to be eliminated. It just did not work that way. I kept an on-going log of all of my musical performances so I would know the last time I played at a certain venue, as well as what I played. The log which I maintain still remains useful today.

Even though I finally developed a repertoire of approximately thirty songs that I liked to play, I found that most of my special requests involved approximately ten songs that I was asked to play regularly. The identification of these songs is rather interesting. Let me list the ten most popular songs that I play:

1.   The most popular song I played as a soloist in my ministry was *"Because He Lives"*, which was the first song I learned to play and still remains the most requested.

2.   In later years, the second most popular song was a fairly new song written by Dr. Beau Williams. That song is *"Show Me the Way"*. I had never heard anyone sing that song before or since for that matter, but for me it became a favorite. Incidentally, Dr. Beau Williams and I both received our Doctor of Divinity Degree from the ITGW theological seminary in 2008.

The other eight songs in my top ten are as follows, in the order of their popularity.

3.   *His Eye is on the Sparrow.*
4.   *At the Cross*
5.   *He Looked beyond My Fault*
6.   *How Great Thou Art*
7.   *Glory to His Name*
8.   *What a Friend we have in Jesus*
9.   *There is a Fountain*
10.   *The Old Rugged Cross*

I had indicated earlier that one of the constraints that I attempted to place on my music ministry was to limit my playing to just one outside performance each month. The Holy Spirit quickly let me know that was not acceptable. I was to *"go where He said I was to go"* and *"do what He said I was to do."* As a consequence and to reaffirm what my mission was, I had to play eight, yes, eight outside engagements in October of 1999, just five months after my wife passed. After that, I knew I needed to let myself be guided by the Holy Spirit. I remember playing in Houston, as well as Atlanta, Georgia during that period. There also were other engagements outside of Central Texas.

After I played approximately one hundred and fifty performances during the 1990s, I begin to suffer from burnout and slowly began to withdraw from the Christian music scene. I would still play locally from time to time, and I even hosted several outdoor musical concerts at my farm, the SWIFT "Two Mile" Farms, near Gause, Texas. These outdoor concerts remained highly popular and the attendance exceeded my fondest expectations. I would simply post notices of the date and time of the concert and advise everyone to bring their own chairs. On some of those occasions I would be joined by other musicians and we would have a grand time.

Throughout my years of steadily performing I only had one inviolable rule that I abided by, I would not take any money for my performances. I felt that God had richly blessed me beyond measure and that I was doing the work that He had set aside for me to do in my community

My Music Ministry

17

CALIFORNIA OR TEXAS, WHICH DO I CHOOSE?

In late 2000 I moved to Inglewood, California to marry Rev. Doctor Media M. Smith and joined the Upper Room Christian Church in Los Angeles, California where she was the Pastor of Women Ministries. I immediately began to work in the church in any capacity the Pastor assigned me to. The Pastor asked me to serve for one year as the Minister of Administration, however, I was willing to work in any capacity. I believe that ALL of the needed chores in our churches or religious congregations are very important and none of them should be beneath our dignity. Jesus gave us an excellent example of this when He stooped down and washed His disciples' feet.

In addition to my other duties at the church I continued to play several times each month in the various services, as well as continue to be invited to play at different community functions. I again particularly targeted those community agencies that served the community's elderly. I found this venue to be very rewarding and was in fact cited by the Los Angeles County Board of Supervisors during Black History Month 2001 for my work in that regard.

In March of 2001 my wife and I moved back to my native state of Texas, but did not return immediately to my music ministry. I played from time to time at my home church, Mount Tabor Baptist, but my passion for music seemed to have escaped me. I no longer felt the anointing that I had previously felt. I again felt that my career as a Christian saxophonist was drawing to a close.

In June of 2002, my wife and I joined the congregation at the Institute for Teaching God's Word and I asked to be permitted to play in the worship services. I was back fully active in my music ministry again and the old level of excitement and sense of fulfillment returned, praise the Lord! I began again to accept outside engagements and play a musical concert monthly at a nursing home in Hearne, Texas. I again felt that I was doing the work that the Lord had set aside for me. Now, let me talk briefly about the next phrase of my life because it became one of great importance.

18

THE ODYSSEY CONTINUES

When my late wife Marjorie was alive and we were living in Austin, I often talked to her about studying in a seminary. Since I was a Sunday School teacher I wanted to know more about the Word of God. The year was now 2002 and I was living full time on my farm in Gause. I heard that there was a small Bible School, or School of Ministry located in Rockdale, Texas, which was only twenty-three miles from my farm, and I had better to do. I went to Rockdale and found the <u>Institute for Teaching God's Word</u> (ITGW) Theological Seminary. It was a non-denominational school and met my needs perfectly.

I already had a Bachelor's Degree in Criminal Justice Administration from the University of Missouri at Kansas City, and a Master's Degree in Criminal Justice Administration from Central Missouri State University in Warrensburg, Missouri. So, I decided that I would pursue another Master's Degree, this time in Biblical Studies at ITGW. I enrolled immediately and began my studies in the fall of 2002. I must admit that looking back, I thought this little Bible school in this little country town was going to be a cake walk.

After all, *I am an alumni of the University of Missouri*, I thought. And this little old school could not be too much of a challenge. I can tell you now that I received the shock of my life and was humbled at ITGW. Though it was small, it was staffed by a faculty of God-fearing, highly capable and very demanding professors. They piled the work on and insisted that we deliver. I began to learn mysteries, the intricacies and the truth in God's Word, almost out of self-defense. Oh how I came to love studying the Word of God! In fact, I would wish that every Christian felt compelled to study God's Word as intensely as we did, since it was only through that intense study of God's Word that His truth opened up to me.

My first year studies of such topics as: the Pentatuch, the Book of Isaiah (a book that I could make no sense out of before the Seminary), Systematic Theology, Spiritual Protocol and Demonology and Deliverance truly opened my eyes to what the apostle Paul was telling the young pastor Timothy at 2nd Timothy 2:15. Let me cite that scripture for you:

> *"Study to show thyself approved unto God, a workman that needeth not be ashamed, rightly dividing the Word of truth. [2nd Timothy 2:15]*

I will give you one example of how stringent the academic requirements were at ITGW. Since I already had a Master's Degree in Criminal Justice, which I worked long and hard to receive, I hated to write research papers. I thought I could sway the ITGW staff to allow me to obtain a Master's Degree without writing another research paper. Right? Wrong! I was told that ALL candidates for the Master's Degree were required to prepare a sixty page thesis, and I was no exception. When I asked for my thesis assignment they gave me the topic of the "The Dead Sea Scrolls". The thesis question I had to address was: *"Do the Dead Sea Scrolls validate the*

Authenticity of the Holy Bible?". I literally fretted about this assignment for an entire month and even considered leaving ITGW. Thank God it was only for a moment. One day as I was reading my Bible I came across Philippians 4:13 which reminded me:

> *"I can do ALL things through Christ which strengtheneth me." [Philippians 4:13]*

What an eye opener this was for me. This God that I serve said that I could do all things through Him. Did I believe that? Did I have the faith in the Word of God that I said I had? If so, WRITE THE THESIS!

During the month of October 2002, it rained for ten straight days here in Central Texas. I had already begun the search of local libraries as well as the internet, gathering up everything that I could find about the Dead Sea Scrolls. Because of the rain I had no distractions to shift my focus and my then wife understood the importance of my journey and was not a cause of distraction either. When the rain subsided, I was finished my thesis with only one slight problem. I had enjoyed writing it so much that when I got to page sixty I could not quit. The final thesis ended up being sixty nine pages long.

By that time I was on fire! I read everything that I could get my hands on and took every class I could take. By the end of 2003 I had earned my Master of Arts Degree in Biblical Studies and on June 4, 2005 I received my Doctor of Ministry in Christian Counseling from the ITGW Seminary. Finally, on December 8, 2008, I received my Doctor of Divinity Degree, also from the ITGW Theological Seminary. At this point I had gotten all of my formal education out of the way.

Along this educational journey, in the 2005-2006 school year, I had been asked to become a member of the teaching staff at ITGW and was assigned to teach Christian Leadership. I also, due to my extensive management and administrative experience, was asked to serve one year as the ITGW Seminary's Provost, which I agreed to do. In 2006, I was asked to become ITGW's President, but I declined. You see, I had found my niche, I wanted to teach! Oh how I enjoyed teaching the Word of God. So, "I" decided that I would spend the rest of my life teaching in the seminary and "that" was all I was going to do. Right? Wrong!

My ministry at Mt. Tabor Baptist Church

19

A NEW YEAR, A NEW WIFE, A NEW JOB

The year 2006 started out for me as a very normal year. I was now teaching as a professor at the ITGW Seminary; I was 70 years old and single once again. My wife and I had different lifestyles - I'm just a country boy and she was a city girl. I previously had moved to California because I wanted to please my wife, not because it was where the Lord told me to be. She then agreed to move to Texas with me for the same reasons, but she was not happy. So once again I was at a crossroads.

When I came back to Texas I moved into one of my sister's, Jessie Cooperwood and her husband L. V.'s houses which was located on the August Long Estate lands. In fact, I was now living less than one hundred feet from where I grew up as a child. I was responsible for handling all of the administrative duties associated with the August Long Estate, and I had just finished negotiating a very lucrative oil and gas contract for all the August Long heirs. I was living in the "Over flow" that I hear my fellow Christians talking about.

I had been praying for another companion, but so far God had not answered that prayer. I was beginning to think that I already had been married too many times. Maybe I was to stay single for the rest of my life. But I also knew that I felt incomplete. And I talked to the Lord and asked Him to give me peace in my present condition, or send me a Help mate.

Things started changing when this little woman showed up in my Church, the New Jerusalem Interdenomination Church of Rockdale, Texas, where I was serving as an Associate Minister. When I say little I mean just that. I have always been attracted to tall, stately women, however she had a petite, small frame. I soon found that she was getting my undivided attention, she intrigued me. I asked around about her and found out she was single. Unfortunately, it was not being reciprocated.

While I was busy trying to get her attention, the Pastor of my original church, Mount Tabor Baptist, resigned and they began looking for a new pastor. Several of the members inquired if I was interested in being the pastor of Mount Tabor. My answer was a resounding NO! Finally, several of the members asked me if I would come and preach a sermon on the 1st Sunday of August (2006). Of course I could not refuse them, but I let them know that I was in no way interested in becoming their pastor. The various solicitations finally got so bad that I promised one of the members that I would pray over it. "That" was only to get him out of my hair. Think about my circumstances, here I was at seventy years old and I had never been the pastor of a church before, nor was I looking for a church to lead. Quite frankly, at seventy years of age, I JUST WANTED TO BE LEFT ALONE!

One day I decided to come before God in prayer, and settle this matter once and for all times. Since I wanted to be sure that I was hearing from God Himself, I asked Him to give me a sign. After all, Gideon asked God for a sign in the book of Judges and God answered him by giving him the sign he asked for. Gideon was so unsure that he asked God for another sign, the opposite of the first one, just to be sure. Again, God gave Gideon what he asked for. Let's look at a part of that story.

> *"And Gideon said unto God, if thou will save Israel by mine hands, as thou hast said, (37) Behold I will put a fleece of wool in the floor; and if the dew be on the fleece only, and it be dry upon all the earth beside, then shall I know that thou will save Israel by mine hand, as thou hath said. (38) And it was so: for he rose up early on the morrow, and thrust the fleece together, and wringed out the dew out of the fleece, a bowl full of water."* [Judges 6:36-38]

I certainly did not believe that God was calling me to pastor Mount Tabor, and I have seen too many church leaders that either call themselves to a leadership position, or allow man to call them. I also teach Christian Leadership at the seminary. In my classes I use Biblical examples of:

- Men who call themselves to positions of headship, and what happens to them. [See the story of Korah at Numbers, 16 Chapter]
- Man appointed leadership. [See King Saul – 1st Samuel]

Of course there are many examples in the Bible where God called such leaders as Moses, Jeremiah, and David - the list is endless. So, here I was not willing to make a mistake in my walk with the Lord. He had watched over me and guided my journey so far, what else should I do? I said Lord, give me a sign.

I remembered something else in God's Word of how He describes Himself. One day Jehovah God told the prophet Malachi this:

"For I am the Lord, I change not;" [Malachi 3:6a]

If you believe in God, it is so beneficial to know what He tells us in His Word. I decided that since God does not change and I had the same right to ask him for a confirmation that Gideon did. So I asked for one and thought, *"This" ought to settle it.*

It was a week or so later, when I got my answer. One morning at approximately 4 or 5AM, I was up reading my Bible, as I had a habit of doing when I woke up early. I remember that I was reading in the 28th chapter of the book of Deuteronomy and I fell back to sleep. My Bible fell to the floor and as I looked down I noticed that it was opened to the 41st chapter of the book of Isaiah, and two of the verses had been highlighted. These verses had been highlighted by me the previous year, for reasons unknown to me. They were verses 9 and 10. As I read them, the hair stood up on the back of my neck. This is what it said: (I am reading from the King James Version.)

"Thou whom I have taken from the ends of the earth, and called thee from the chief men thereof, and said unto thee, Thou art My servant; I have chosen thee, and not cast thee away. (10) Fear thou not; for I am with thee: Be not dismayed; for I am thy God: I will strengthened thee; yea, I will help thee; yea, I will uphold thee with the right hand of My righteousness." [Isaiah 41: 9-10]

I sat silently, stunned and all that I could say was, "Yes Lord". I then knew I was going to be the next pastor of the church that played such an important role in my family, the church of my grandfather and of my mother, the Mount Tabor Baptist Church. WOW!

I turned seventy on August 11, 2006, and Mount Tabor's members asked if I would come in and be interviewed on August 12th. Since I already knew the outcome I was not apprehensive. Later that day, the Deacon came by my house and advised me that the committee of seven members voted me as their next pastor. I am not sure what I felt at that time, but I knew that I would work hard at being a pastor. I wanted to be the best Pastor they had ever had and I wanted to teach them the "TRUTH" in the Word of God.

I now had another problem which was that I was unmarried, but thought I had a quick solution to that problem. Although I was still interested in the new lady that I mentioned previously, I wanted to be obedient and I wanted the Lord to deliver my mate to me. I went back before the Lord in prayer. I found out that her name was Margie and she was a member of the Mack family members who resided in Rockdale. She had become very friendly, but still seemed to be leery of marriage to an "old codger" like me. Margie was also on the ministry staff at the New Jerusalem church in Rockdale where I too was serving.

I learned that she had five grown children and from all that I could tell, she was an outstanding mother. That was important to me because I needed someone to help me "mother" those "old children" of mine. My first wife, Pearl Swift, passed at the young age of fifty-four and although we were divorced and I had remarried a couple of times, we grew into a friendship that was special to me. My children were very attached to their mother and although no one could ever replace her, they had a void.

In my prayer, I asked the Lord to send me a Help mate. I told the Lord that I would serve Him under any circumstances, but I preferred to have a wife who could help me minister more effectively to the women members of Mount Tabor. I told the Lord that He knew the one that I preferred, but if she was not the one, I asked that He take my desire for her away. After I made that request before the Lord, my relationship to Margie seemed to have changed almost overnight. We were married in October of 2006. Her presence in my life has continued to make my walk with my Lord and Savior Jesus Christ a joy beyond my comprehension.

20

FRUITS OF THE SPIRIT

I am now completing my fifth year of being the pastor of the Mount Tabor Baptist Church in Gause, Texas. There is no way that I could have fathomed how much joy and spiritual fulfillment I have had serving as pastor of this church. I know now that God placed in me something that I didn't know was in me. After all of those years of being a police officer, in all kind of assignments, serving as a pastor has changed me for the rest of my life.

I have had plenty of experience as a father, a grandfather, and even a great grandfather. I also knew how to function as a servant, although not always a good one. But what I have learned during these past five years is how to be a "Shepherd". Jesus Christ is our Great Shepherd and He has set an example for all Christian leaders. It is not necessarily an easy job, however, my hope is that one day you too will be as blessed as I have been and will aspire to be a shepherd to others. Again, Jesus Christ is the Great Shepherd. He:

- Searched – for those who were lost

- Delivered - those who were captives

- <u>Fed</u> – those who were hungry

- <u>Gathered</u> – those who had wandered astray, and

- <u>Guided</u> – those who had lost their direction

Much of the hardness that I had experienced as a police officer is gone and has been replaced by a gentleness that I did not have before becoming a Pastor, a Shepherd. I now understand what the apostle Paul was talking about in his letter to the Galatians when he spoke of the "Fruit of the Spirit." He said:

> *"But the fruit of the Spirit is love, joy, peace, longsuffering, gentleness, goodness, faith, (23) meekness, temperance: against such there is no law." [Galatians 5:22-23]*

My daughter reminded me that when I first started in my search for the true God, I challenged my children to know what the fruitage of the spirit was. None of them were aware of these Godly qualities. That was the first spiritual truths I embedded into their hearts and she says that to this very day she reminds herself of Galatians 5:22-23 daily. I guess the Lord knew that for me to persevere, I too would have to dwell on those words.

21

A SPIRIT OF GIVING

When I began studying at the ITGW Seminary, I was blessed by a special person that God placed in my path, a man that I have a great deal of love and affection for. That individual is Dr. Dennis L. Brooks, PHD, who is the Founder and President of the ITGW Theological Seminary. He was one of my theological professors, as well as the Pastor of the New Jerusalem Church which I attend.

I knew practically nothing about the Word of God when I began my studies under Dr. Brooks at the seminary. He became my mentor, as well as a spiritual father. I studied under both he and his wife, Dr. Clara Brooks, and found them both to be excellent, although demanding instructors, whose godly gifts were opening up closed minds to let the flow of God's truth come in. And although my aspirations weren't always to become a theologian, I thank God for Dr. Brooks' presence in my life and I am eternally grateful for his teachings. I consider him to be another one of my "heroes" (even thought he would be surprised that I thought of him in that way) for he has made a great impact on my life and my Odyssey. Today, I continue to serve as a professor at the Institute for Teaching God's Word Theological Seminary in Rockdale, Texas where my wife and I now reside. In addition to Christian Leadership, I also teach Apologetics, which teaches Christians how to defend their faith.

A special gift that God has given me

There has been another aspect of my life that has been quite a joy and a blessing to me which I want to share with everyone. That is the fact that I have, as long as I can remember, experienced a sense of great joy and satisfaction when I have been able to give to or assist those in need. Looking back I am sure that this was one of the examples my grandfather, August Long, set for me. I did not think much of it when I was younger became that is the way I was raised. However, as I matured, I noticed the pleasure and sense of satisfaction whenever I could give of my services and especially of my finances. Over the years I have given thousands and thousands of dollars because I felt that as Jehovah God had blessed me mightily over the years, I needed to share with those in need. I even gave when I really did not have it to give. But, if I thought that the other person's needs were greater than my own, I gave.

Let me share one of the instances of giving in which looking back, I am not proud of. When I was living in Austin one day my late wife and I were driving around the city when I saw a man standing on a corner with a sign saying that he needed bus fare to get home. I forget where he said he lived but it was within fifty miles of Austin. I reached my hand into my pocket and pulled out a ten dollar bill and gave it to him. I told him I knew that was more than enough, but I wanted him to be able to buy something to eat. I felt good about giving freely and knew it was what I was supposed to do. Imagine my surprise when several hours later I happened to drive by that same bus stop and the same man was still there holding up the same sign. Angrily, I pulled over, got out of my car and made him give me my ten dollars back. After I drove off my wife made the comment that as a Christian, if I gave from my heart I had fulfilled my Christian responsibility and I should let God deal with the man, not me. I have never forgotten that wonderful lesson.

My wife Margie has a similar desire to give to those in need, so we make a perfect team in our giving. Each year, after we have paid a tenth of our income to our church, (we believe in paying our "tithes" because we believe that God's Word requires it), we fund other charitable organizations which assist people in need all over the world. In a recent typical year we supported feeding and sending several children in the Philippines to school, fully funded the opening of a medical clinic in the mountains of Haiti and supported a missionary organization which serves South and Central American countries. Funding missionary organizations should not come as a surprise when one understands that my wife, Margie, loves to work on the foreign mission fields at every opportunity. Sadly, she is not able to do so now because she is working on her Master's degree at the ITGW seminary where I teach.

You may ask yourself why this idea of giving and helping others is so important. It is not until one understands that giving and serving should be the cornerstone of a Christian's lifestyle and is a special gift that is given to us by God's Holy Spirit. We are rewarded by using this gift. I'm not speaking of material rewards, I am speaking of spiritual rewards. Our giving should not be conditional, as Jesus' most precious gift to us had no conditions upon it. Jesus lets us know that when we give and do for others, we are giving and doing for Him. There are many scriptural passages that confirm this fact. Jesus taught his disciples in the 25th Chapter of the book of Matthew the following: [NOTE: Bible published by The Gideons International]

> *"Then the King (Jesus) will say to those on His right hand, 'Come, you blessed of My Father, inherit the kingdom prepared for you from the foundation of the world: (35) for I was hungry and you gave Me food: I was thirsty and you gave me drink; I was a stranger and you took Me in; (36) I was naked and you clothed Me; I was sick and you visited Me; I was in prison and you came to Me." [Matthew 25:34-36]*

When Jesus spoke to his followers about this they were puzzled because they had never treated him in such a fashion. When they questioned Jesus about this (verses 37 – 39), Jesus' answer to them should be very instructive to all of us:

> *"And the King (Jesus) will answer and say to them, 'Assuredly I say to you, as you did it to one of the least of these My brethren, you did it to Me."*
> *[Matthew 25:40]*

2011 – My wife, Margi and me visiting my nephew Anthony

22

AN EXCITING ADVENTURE

As I was writing this letter I received notification that my nephew, my sister Jessie's son, was going to be in a city near us. Anthony, who is a world class musician and has played jazz and other instruments all over the world, is currently a musician with the world famous Cirque Du Soleil "Dralion". Since he and his family live in Montreal, Canada I don't get a chance to see him too often. Anthony is an excellent example of what I spoke about at the beginning of this letter. He has wanted to be a musician since he was a little kid and his parents, L. V. and Jessie Cooperwood, supported his desire in every way they could. I remember when he was young and first began taking piano lessons. The family had no piano but that did not stop Anthony from practicing his lessons. He would finger each note position he had been taught by his teacher on any flat surface he could find - books, table tops, or the coffee table, anything. His parents had to hurry up and buy him a piano. He later studied music at my old school, the University of Missouri at Kansas City, and eventually earned a full musical scholarship to Northeast Missouri State University (NMSU) where he ultimately earned a Bachelor of Arts Degree in Music, a Bachelor of Arts Degree in

Piano Performance and a Masters in Music Education. I cite Anthony as an example of what we can all be if we decide to work hard for what we want to be in life. As I said before, if you are willing to work hard, "the sky is the limit".

Margie and I certainly enjoyed the fantastic show and afterwards, since we were guests of Anthony's, we were able to go back behind stage and see how this show was put together and meet some of the performers. Anthony had one of his friends to take a picture of Anthony, Margie, the "Dralion" (think "Dragon + Lion) and me. We certainly had a wonderful time. After spending the night, we came back to Rockdale so I could get ready for the Bible Study that I am currently teaching, and to finish this letter.

23

I WAS LOST, NOW I'M FOUND

My dear loved ones, I hope that you will keep this information and pass it along to your kids, my off-springs. God has blessed me to enjoy such a full and wonderful life in this world that we call the Earth. Moreover, Jehovah God "found" me, as He will find each of you if you are willing to be found by Him. I am so thankful that he waited on me as I came to my senses. But, the Word of God has explained why He did. We see the explanation of this in two scriptures in God's Word. One day these scriptures may give you the hope that I found. I will use the New Living Translation Bible.

> *"For God loved the world so much that He gave His one and only Son, so that everyone who believes in Him will not perish, but have everlasting life."*
> *[John 3:16]*

> *"The Lord isn't really slow about His promise, as some people think. No, He is being patient for your sake. He does not want anyone to be destroyed, but He wants everyone to repent."*
> *[2 Peter 3:9]*

I thank God that He waited on me to come to my senses and accept Jesus Christ as my Lord and Savior. Looking back, I want to thank Jehovah God for placing several people in my life that played a major part making me the Man of God that I am, and played an important part in the successes in my life. I call them my personal "Heroes." My mother, Juanita Long Swift, is not listed because I take that for granted. Being the oldest child, I guess that I always had a special relationship with her. One of the things that was so helpful to me growing up was, I did not care what it was, I COULD TALK TO MY MAMA ABOUT IT. We remained that way until she went home to glory in 1983. The remainder of these special people that God placed in my life I will list in the order in which they touched my life.

- August Long, my Maternal Grandfather

- Mrs. Lois Plummer, my High School Math Teacher

- 1st Lieutenant Homer Petite, my Communications Commander

- Alvin Brooks, my Trainer at the Kansas City Missouri Police Department

- Clarence M. Kelley, Chief of the Kansas City, Missouri Police Department, and

- Dr. Dennis L. Brooks, PHD, my Seminary Professor and friend

No words can describe the impact that these "Heroes" have had upon my life. Even though several were in my life briefly, they made the difference. My hope is that somewhere along the way I *will* and *have* made such a difference in someone's life.

My children, let me close this overview of my life, by leaving you with some "Food for thought." As we look around us it is clear that we are living in perilous and troubled times. God's Word tells us exactly what mankind will see and experience in what the Word of God refers to as the "latter days". When Jesus' followers asked Him about what would be the signs of the coming of those times, Jesus' response is recorded in the 24th chapter of Matthew. Let me cite a portion of that warning here. It may be lengthy but when you understand this scriptural passage, you will have a better understanding of the events that are unfurling before our eyes. Most of the world has no clue, yet this warning has been before us all of these years. I will again use my favorite modern English translation, the New Living Translation, Matthew 24:3-14:

> *"Later Jesus sat on the Mount of Olives. His disciples came to Him privately and said, "tell us, when will all this happen? What sign will signal your return and the end of the world?"*

> *(4) Jesus told them, "don't let anyone mislead you,*

> *(5) for many will come in My name, claiming, 'I am the Messiah. They will deceive many.*

> *(6) And you will hear of wars and threats of wars, but don't panic. Yes, these things must take place, but the end won't follow immediately.*

> *(7) Nation will go to war against nation, and kingdom against kingdom. There will be famines and earthquakes in many parts of the world.*

> *(8) But all this is only the first of the birth pains, with more to come.*

(9) Then you will be arrested, persecuted and killed. You will be hated all over the world because you are my followers.

(10) And many will turn away from me and betray and hate each other.

(11) And many false prophets will appear and deceive many people.

(12) Sin will be rampant everywhere, and the love of many will grow cold.

(13) But the one who endures to the end will be saved.

(14) And the Good News about the Kingdom will be preached throughout the whole world, so that all nations will hear it; and then the end will come;"

Now let me close my letter to you with a prayer that I pray most days for the welfare of our country, its people and its leaders. I do this because the Word of God requires this of Christians. You can find that instruction at 1st Timothy 2:1-3 which tells us to:

"I urge you first of all, to pray for all people. Ask God to help them; intercede on their behalf, and give thanks for them. (2) Pray this way for kings and all who are in authority so that we can live peaceful and quiet lives marked by godliness and dignity. (3) This is good and pleases God our Savior"
[1st Timothy 2:1-3] New Living Translation

PRAYER

HEAVENLY FATHER, OUR GRAND AND GRACIOUS CREATOR, I COME BEFORE YOU THIS HOUR WITH <u>LOVE</u> AND <u>ADORATION</u> IN HEART AND I COME IN A SPIRIT OF <u>HUMILITY</u> AND <u>OBEDIENCE</u>.

I COME, LORD, THIS HOUR CONCERNED ABOUT THE FUTURE OF OUR NATION, THESE UNITED STATES OF AMERICA. AND I AM PRAYING TODAY FOR THE WELFARE AND THE PEOPLE OF OUR NATION AND, AS YOU REQUIRE IN YOUR WORD, I AM PRAYING FOR THOSE THAT HATE US AND DESPITEFULLY MISUSE US. AND I AM PRAYING FOR THOSE WHO ABUSE US AND PERSECUTE US. I AM EVEN PRAYING FOR THOSE THAT COME AGAINST OUR NATION, BOTH FROM <u>WITHIN</u> IT'S BORDERS AS WELL AS FROM <u>THE OUTSIDE</u>. AND I ASK THAT YOU, THROUGH YOUR LOVE, GRACE AND MERCY WILL CHANGE THEM. I PRAY LORD THAT OUR NATION WILL CHANGE FOR THE BETTER IN YOUR EYESIGHT. AND I AM PRAYING FOR OUR PRESIDENT AND THE LEADERSHIP OF OUR NATION.

LORD - YOU SAY IN YOUR WORD AT (JAMES 5:16) THAT "THE EFFECTUAL FERVENT PRAYER OF A RIGHTEOUS MAN AVAILETH MUCH AND YOUR SON, JESUS CHRIST, OUR LORD AND OUR SAVIOUR, TAUGHT US THAT IF WE HAD FAITH, AND HAD NO DOUBT IN OUR HEARTS, AND IF WE ASKED IN PRAYER FOR ANYTHING IN HIS NAME, "HAVING THAT <u>FAITH</u>" WE WOULD RECEIVE IT. (JOHN 16: 23-24)

LORD, YOU HAVE SET OUR PRESIDENT OVER THIS GREAT NATION OF OURS...

- THIS NATION THAT FROM ITS BEGINNING ACKNOWLEDGED THAT IT BELONGED TO YOU;

130

- THIS NATION THAT WE DESCRIBE, AS ONE NATION UNDER GOD, INDIVISIBLE, WITH LIBERTY AND JUSTICE FOR ALL;

- THIS NATION THAT FROM ITS INFANCY, FROM IT'S BEGINNING, YOU HAVE BLESSED BEYOND MEASURE, AND

I KNOW LORD THAT YOU HAVE PROMISED WE, YOUR PEOPLE, THROUGH YOUR PROPHETS, THAT IF WE BRING OUR LIVES INTO HARMONY WITH <u>YOUR WILL</u>, WITH <u>YOUR WAYS</u>, AND WITH <u>YOUR WORD</u>, THAT YOU ARE GOING TO BLESS OUR NATION AGAIN IN A VERY SPECIAL WAY. AND AS YOU PROMISED YOUR SERVANT, THE PROPHET ISAIAH, AT (ISAIAH 54:17) THAT NO WEAPON FORMED AGAINST YOUR SERVANT SHALL PROSPER, I AM PRAYING LORD THAT NO <u>HURT</u> - NO <u>HARM</u> - NOR <u>DANGER</u> BEFALL THE LEADERSHIP OF OUR NATION.

I PRAY, O GREAT JEHOVAH-SHALOME, THAT OUR LEADERS LEAD OUR NATION INTO <u>PEACE</u> AND I PRAY THAT YOU AWAKEN IN "US", YOUR SONS & DAUGHTERS, A FERVENT SPIRITUALITY THAT FOCUSES UPON "YOU" AND THAT WE PROSPER AS A NATION, EVEN AS YOUR WORD TELLS US THAT OUR SOUL PROSPERS.

LORD, I PRAY THAT OUR PRESIDENT'S LEADERSHIP WILL FOSTER <u>PEACE</u>, <u>UNITY</u> AND <u>TRANQUILITY</u> AMONG YOUR PEOPLE IN A WAY THAT IS PLEASING IN YOUR EYESIGHT. AND I PRAY THAT OUR NATION WILL TURN ITSELF BACK TO YOU. I PRAY THAT WE, YOUR PEOPLE, WILL LIFT OUR NATION UP BEFORE YOU IN PRAYER AND THAT YOU WOULD USE OUR NATION'S LEADERSHIP AS AN INSTRUMENT OF YOUR WILL, AND THAT THEY WILL PREPARE THIS GREAT NATION OF OURS

FOR THE NEW SPIRITUAL AWAKENING THAT YOU HAVE PROMISED US. NOW LORD, WE GIVE YOU LOVE, WE GIVE YOU THE PRAISE AND WE GIVE YOU THE GLORY. IN THE MIGHTY NAME OF YOUR SON, OUR LORD AND OUR SAVIOUR JESUS CHRIST. **AMEN!**

If I had to leave you, my loved ones, and I was only permitted to leave you with one piece of advice, I would have to turn to the Word of God again. I will do so by quoting a portion of two scriptures. King David taught his son Solomon:

> *"And Solomon, my son, learn to know the God of your ancestors intimately. Worship and serve Him with your whole heart and a willing mind. For the Lord sees every heart and knows every plan and thought.*
>
> *IF YOU SEEK HIM, YOU WILL FIND HIM, BUT IF YOU FORSAKE HIM, HE WILL REJECT YOU FOREVER." [1ST Chronicles 28:9]*

Jehovah God told the prophet Jeremiah:

> *"For I know the plans that I have for you, says the Lord. They are plans for good and not for disaster, to give you a future and a hope. (12). In those days when you pray, I will listen. (13) If you look for Me whole-heartedly, you will find Me. (14) I WILL BE FOUND BY YOU, SAYS THE LORD..."*
> *[Jeremiah 29:11-14a]*

God's Word applies to all of us. We are His creations and He has great plans for each of us, BUT WE MUST SEEK A RELATIONSHIP WITH HIM, and He will bless us mightily.

Love, Granny PaPa

PS: After I finished this letter, the Holy Spirit gave me one final thought to share with you. It concerns something that happened to me back in the 1990s. At that time in my walk with Christ I felt overburdened. So I prayed and asked, "why me?" I felt that even in my greater family's business, it looked like the bulk of the burden fell upon me. I now know the answer. I was reading in the Book of Luke and read the following scripture. I then knew that Jehovah God was answering my question of "Why Me."

*"As it is written in the law of the Lord, 'Every male
that opens the womb shall be called holy to the
Lord." [Luke 2:23]*

God's Word tells us that the first child born to a woman is the one that opens her womb for the first time, whether male or female, God has set that one apart for His special purposes. That does not mean that others are not set aside, it means, by the reason of your being the first born of a woman...YOU ARE SPECIAL TO GOD! He has a special assignment for you.

As a result of being my mother's firstborn, I ended up being the leader of my family. You may think that this is a position of great power and strength, but Jesus taught us that we lead by being a servant. Yes, I have learned to be a servant to my family, to my church and to my community. The scripture that I quoted said, 'as it is written in the law of the Lord". You may want to look at some of the Old Testament scriptures on this. Let me list a few for you:

- Exodus 13:2
- Numbers 3:13, and
- Deuteronomy 15

I love you madly!

APPENDIX

MY CHOCTOW HERITAGE

As I thought about my deep Choctaw, I was moved to research my heritage. There was so much I did not know. I also didn't know where to start, and thought maybe I should start by contacting some of my relatives in the Oklahoma City area, like Sherman White, and have him, or someone to help me find out something about the Choctaw Indians and their history. The more that I considered this approach, the less I liked the idea. I had decided that I wanted to write a brief "note" about our forefathers, the Choctaws, so that I could pass this information out at the Long Family Reunion. I thought this would be good information for our younger generations (who most, incidentally, have no knowledge about their Choctaw heritage). They would then become familiar with this part of our family's ancestral history.

It was also a fact, that I only had slightly less than two weeks to gather up what information that I could. So, I decided to do my own research on the internet and develop a brief history...maybe just barely scratching the surface....of Choctaw Indian history. I do not even want to talk about the many "misconceptions" that I already had concerning my Indian forefathers, the Choctaws. For example, I thought that out of the more than 200 named Indian tribes that existed during the 1700s and 1800s, the Choctaw was some minor, insignificant, tribe about which very little had been noted. (Boy, wouldn't my Oklahoma cousins have found that idea hilarious!)

There was however, as I found out, a significant fact that I was aware of, that I was able to verify. My grandmother Saddlewhite was from the Alabama /Mississippi area of the United

States. And that is where I had been told the Choctaws were from. Now, a little bit about what I found.

The Choctaw Indian Tribe, is believed to have originated from the ancient Mexican Empire. The Indian Tribes now known as the Choctaws and the Chickasaws was at one time a single tribe. They emigrated into what is now known as the United States, and crossed to the east side of the Mississippi River. For reasons unknown to historians, the group split into two tribes, and became distinctly different. It was also believed that the Choctaws were distantly related to the Creeks and Seminoles.

Contrary to my original belief, the Choctaw Indians was a very large and powerful tribe. At the height of their power in the south the Choctaw Indian tribe occupied and controlled most of what would later become the southern two-thirds of Mississippi, much of the Mississippi Delta, and parts of what is now western Alabama, and Louisiana.

The Choctaw culture was strictly "matriarchal," (meaning dominated by the females). Any discussion of Choctaw ancestry begins with the knowledge that the greater prestige in Choctaw ancestry begins with an understanding of the family tree of the Choctaw mother, and Choctaw grandmother, great grandmother, etc.

Most Choctaws lived in villages since this arrangement provided mutual protection as well as other advantages. The Choctaw mother spent most of her time at the village, giving birth and rearing the children. The farm plot of maize, beans and other crops were also her responsibility and those of her minor children. (Sounds like a description of the "Virtuous Woman" found in Proverbs 31). An interesting fact: If a Choctaw mother had

135

problems with one of her sons, she turned not to his biological father, but to her oldest brother or to the village elder for help.

A Choctaw brave's contact with his children was only incidental and he bore no responsibility for the rearing of his children!! Members of both sexes practiced polygamy, but it was most often the male who had more than one spouse, with each one living in a different village. The primary role of the Choctaw adult male was those of <u>hunter</u> and <u>protector</u>. He often spent more time in the forest and fields hunting than he did at the village. He followed game on a seasonal basis, and therefore had to relocate his camps often. Even traveling primarily by foot, the Choctaw Indian brave was known to travel as far north as Georgia, Kentucky, and even Missouri in search of materials from which to make their arrowheads and spears.

Let's "fast forward" to 1786. The Choctaw tribe made their first "Treaty" with the United States. And as far as I can tell, never went to war against the United States again! During the 1800s the U.S. Government created an "Indian Territory" in what is now the eastern part of the State of Oklahoma. The government began to "uproot the Indians tribes from their homes east of the Mississippi in a series of federally legislated orders, forcing the Indian tribes to move to this "Indian Territory."

Five of these Indian tribes, were considered by the U.S. Government as "Civilized," and was granted the opportunity to establish their own "Nations" within the "Indian Territory." These tribes were the Cherokee, Chickasaw, Choctaw, Creek, and Seminole. They were considered "civilized" by white society because they had adopted many of the white man's customs, and they generally had good relationships with their neighbors. In these Indian "Nations" they were allowed to establish their own governmental body. So, the Choctaw Nation had its own autonomous government until 1906 when they were admitted to American citizenship and the "Indian Territory" became a part of the State of "Oklahoma."

Since this is to be just a brief "overview" of the history of some of our ancestral people, I want to discuss one other aspect of the Choctaws before I close. That is the fact that many of the Choctaw Indians had black slaves!! Let me quote from one of the documents that I read:

"Brought to Indian Territory in the 1830's Black Choctaws arrived with the Choctaw Indians as slaves. Prior to removal the Choctaws had been exposed to Africans in their native homeland of Mississippi. Slaves were a part of the European culture to which the Choctaws would later adapt."

The only black family of distinct free status in the Choctaw Nation at the time of the removal to the Indian Territory was the Beams family, children of Nellie Beams. Slavery remained in the Choctaw Nation until 1866, when the treaty of 1866 signed in Fort Smith, Arkansas required that The Choctaws release their African slaves from bondage.

Most "Freedmen" remained in the Choctaw Nation, and began new lives as citizens among their Indian neighbors. It appears, however, that once the Blacks were free....Many of the Choctaws did not want them to remain. The following comments appeared in one of the documents that I read. "Much discussion arose in the nation after the signing of the Treaty, and many in the nation had pressed to have the Freemen removed from the Choctaw Nation. However, a majority of the Freemen remained steadfast, determined to remain in the land of their birth, as law abiding Choctaw citizens..."

Finally, after much discussion, debates, and years of political strategizing, in 1885, the Choctaw Nation finally adopted their former slaves as citizens into the nation. This new status gave them a legal right to remain and no longer be considered as "intruders" in the land of their birth.

As I close out this research, I find myself wanting to begin to talk about some of the legacies that these Black Choctaw Freemen left behind....BUT..."that" is not within the scope of this research. So let me close by doing two things. First, as a career law enforcement officer, let me say that two of the prominent law enforcement officers to come of that time and place were black men of distinction. One, Rufus Cannon, served the Indian Territory as a U. S. Marshall. Another noted black law enforcement officer of that period was Deputy Sheriff Squire Hall. Sheriff served with great distinction!! Let me close at this point.

Now, in according with a Choctaw tradition...I will pick for myself a Choctaw name which, in my thinking, describes who I am. I am choosing the following:

Holahta: "Leader"

Kannakli: "Moves Quickly" (SWIFT!!)

So my new Choctaw name is translated as "Leader of the Swifts". That is all. Hope you enjoy any parts of this, and just remember...Choctaw blood runs richly through our veins!!

LOVE,

Holahta Kannakli

SOME OF MY THOUGHTS ON ABORTION

Nothing has grieved me more in the past thirty or so years, than the senseless slaughter of our Nation's unborn children via abortions. I have found it so difficult to stomach the idea that this great Nation of ours, which presumable was founded upon Christian principles, would allow this "mockery" or moral justice to be perpetrated upon its people.

I used to just agonize about this thing we call abortion, but one day I awaken and found myself to be a Bible Teacher and a Minister and decided I had a moral obligation to try to open the "spiritual eyes" of others, hopefully to make them realize that abortion was the killing of a human being, and that Jehovah God, The Creator of all human life, would hold us accountable as a Nation one day.

This idea of my country sanctioning the legalizing of abortion, because the unborn fetus is not "viable", causes so many memories in my life to swirl away in my mind, and I just don't understand how we have arrived at this "place" that permits this great so-called "Christian Nation" of ours to not SEE and UNDERSTAND that abortion is a violation of one of God's Ten Commandments that tells us that "THOU SHALL NOT KILL:.

I REMEMBER: When I was a young child my mother purchased an incubator. We would take some of the eggs that our chickens had laid and Mama would place them in that incubator and light the heat source which was in the center. Every few days Mama would open the incubator and turn all of the eggs so that they faced the heat source equally. In about a month (I think it was 28 days) those little chicks would begin to hatch.

I REMEMBER: As a young man I wondered about whether or not there were any similarities between the creation of those little chicks and the creation of a human baby. And,

I REMEMBER: When I was a young police Sergeant on the Kansas City Missouri Police Department struggling to quell the disturbances during the civil disobedience riots, that I had read Civil Rights Leader, Dr. Martin Luther King, Jr. had written about "just" and "unjust" laws.

In April of 1963 while Dr. King was in the Birmingham jail in Alabama, the local clergymen had been very critical of his involvement in leading the demonstrators in their acts of civil disobedience, and the clergymen wanted to know why he would do such a thing. Dr. King wrote what is now a very famous letter from his jail cell. That letter is called "Letter From A Birmingham Jail". I just want to repeat how Dr. King answered his critics about not obeying an "unjust" law.

Remember, I am repeating Dr. King's remarks because many Christians, in the case of abortion, hide behind the U. S. Supreme Court's decision "ROE VS WADE" because they say it is the law.

DR. KING'S RESPONSE WENT LIKE THIS:

"The answer lies in the fact that there are two types of laws; just and unjust. I would be the first to advocate obeying just laws. One has not only a legal, but a moral responsibility to obey just laws. Conversely, one has a moral responsibility to disobey unjust law. Now, what is the difference between the two? How does one determine whether a law is just or unjust? A just law is a man made code that squares with the moral law, or the law of God. An unjust law is a code that is out of harmony with the moral law."

I wanted to preface my thoughts about why I am so concerned about our Nation's response to this tragedy that is called abortion, and for my children. Here are a few of my thoughts on abortion. What I have done is taken several excerpts from a Bible study that I taught at several Central Texas Churches back in 2004 – 2006. I will call that <u>ABORTION PART 1</u>. PART 2 will be taken from a speech that I delivered to a men's group, also here in Central Texas in 2011.

<u>PART 1</u>

"Thou shall not kill." [Exodus 20:13 "...and the innocent and righteous slay thy not;" [Exodus 23:7]

I was listening to my radio one day some years ago, when I was living in Austin, Texas, when I heard a prominent Pastor of a local church say that one the abortion issue, he was pro-choice. He felt that a woman out to be able to do with her body as she pleases. I cringed at the thought that his parishioners, as well as many people out there in radio land, were being led astray by his nonsensical, ill-formed and uninformed understanding about God's requirements of us. And I asked myself the question, "Has he bothered to read what God's Word has to say on this matter?" Obviously he had considered this matter before he preached it from the pulpit, but how did he come to his conclusion?

Years later I came to understand that many Christian leaders are pro-choice. They say that God's Word does not speak clearly to this issue and, while that is beyond my comprehension, my purpose here is simply to give you some facts and thoughts on this issue, to assist you in making up your own mind.

One of the major issues that I hear people debating over today is abortion. Is it okay or not? Many times when I pick up a magazine or news periodical, I am bombarded by articles taking one view or another. This country is divided into two camps over this issue. One camp is called Pro-Life, and their position is, for simplification, abortions are murder! The opposing position is that a woman ought to be able to do anything that she wishes with her body, including aborting her fetus if she so desires.

The debate over this issue has been so intense until the issue was taken to the Supreme Court, which was decided in 1973, in Roe vs. Wade. It is still such a contentious issue that candidates for political office, including candidates for the Presidency of the United States, may be elected or defeated based on his/her belief on the subject. In my opinion, God's Word is very clear on this subject. It simply says, "THOU SHALL NOT KILL". And it is referring to not killing a human life. There is no doubt that the life of a human, which is the product of Jehovah God, begins at the moment of conception. Critical components of this debate hinges around the question of "at what point does life begin?" They talk about the "viability" of the unborn fetus, and they place great importance on whether the fetus is viable or not.

I want to pause here and provide a definition for this word viable, or viability. The original meaning of this word was "capable of growing or developing". When applied to the human fetus, however, now it has taken on a new meaning, which I believe is ordained by Satan himself. It now means, in a legalistic sense, "capable of surviving outside the mother's womb without any artificial support". Let's talk about this, but first we need to ask ourselves some questions.

Human "Creation" Cycle:

- A live male seed "joins" a live female egg (conception)
- Therefore, at the moment of conception is that organism in the womb "dead or alive?

- If it is dead, at the moment of conception. can life come forth?
- If it is alive, what is it? Human...animal.... plant .... What is it?
- Then if you destroy whatever this is, what have you destroyed?

This subject had puzzled me so much that I sought a better understanding from the Holy Spirit through prayer. One day when I lived in Bryan, Texas, I was out on my daily walk when the Holy Spirit showed me my answer. When a voice inside of me asked the following question:

"HAVE YOU CONSIDERED
THE METAMORPOSIS OF A BUTTERFLY?"

I knew that this was the Holy Spirit prompting me to think about the butterfly to better understand the question I had been asking myself. I understood immediately! Let me share this with you so that you can see the revelation I had just received. I will make it short and none technical:

- When an adult butterfly lays an egg, it is both "alive" and is in fact the beginning of a butterfly. Just like those chicken eggs mama placed in the incubator.
- Later, the butterfly's eggs turn into a caterpillar. Well, is it now not a butterfly? Yes, the butterfly's eggs can only produce a butterfly. The caterpillar therefore is just a butterfly in the making.
- Then the caterpillar changes into something else before finally turning into a live butterfly.

I know understand two things. (1) At each stage in the process, the butterfly was being evolved from the egg through various changes until it ultimately emerged as an adult butterfly. (2) Throughout this process of changing, the butterfly was always alive. Just like mama's chicken eggs, which ultimately became baby chicks.

What then about this "viability" that the U. S. Supreme Court, in Roe vs. Wade ruled, that at some point the human fetus was not "viable", which suggests that the unborn human fetus was not a living human being. Let's look at what the Word of God has to say about these unborn fetuses, or even what God has to say about the unborn before they are conceived. Even before the moment of conception, God knows you!

> *"Then the word of the Lord came unto me, saying, Before I formed thee in the belly, I knew thee; and before thou camest forth out of the womb I sanctified thee, and I ordained thee a prophet unto the nations." [Jeremiah 1:4-5]*

How did God form Jeremiah in his mother's belly? At what point did that forming process begin? Yeah, you got it, at the moment of conception! And that is Jehovah God's creation in that womb. God chose the woman's womb as an "incubator" for the development of, long before the child comes forth into the world.

> *"Listen, O isles, unto me; and hearken, ye people, from far; The Lord hath called me from the womb; from the bowels of my mother hath He made mention of my name." [Isaiah 49:1 also see Isa. 49:5]*

> *"For Thou hast possessed my reins: Thou hast covered me in my mother's womb"...For I am fearfully and wonderfully made:...My substance was not hid from Thee, when I was made in secret,"...Thine eyes did see my substance, yet being unperfect;..." [Psalm 139:13-16 Excerpts]*

<u>DID YOU KNOW</u>: At the moment of conception…

- The developing child has all 23 pairs of its chromosomes
- It's sex has been decided
- Its DNA established, and
- It's hereditary traits have already been established in its DNA

Roe v. Wade is the law of the land? You say!!! We must obey it? Roe vs. Wade is a law that does not square with God's moral law of "Thy Shall not kill."

NOTE: Roe v. Wade was a Civil Rights case. It was not a case about Life or Death at all. It was ruled that a woman had a right to "PRIVACY" to what she did with her own body!!

NOTE: This case was decided on the merits of the Ninth Amendment to the Constitution of the United States. It might prove to be interesting if you read it!!

I have sometimes wondered what Thomas Jefferson was thinking as he was writing the U.S. Declaration of Independence when he wrote the following words:

"We hold these truths to be self-evident, that all men are created equal, that they are endowed by their Creator with certain unalienable Rights, that among these are Life, Liberty and the pursuit of Happiness."

These words have been called "the most potent and consequential words in the history of America". Yet even though all Americans have been endowed by our Creator, Jehovah God, with these special rights, which by the definition of "unalienable" cannot be given nor taken away, nonetheless, our nation has taken it upon itself to turn a blind eye and a deaf ear to millions of humans in America because of this misguided law.

145

Sadly, millions of unborn children have been denied "life, liberty and the pursuit of happiness" because we, in our country, have the legally sanctioned right to snuff out their lives before they are born.

PART 2

These are some brief notes from a speech where I talked on several biblical subjects, including some statistical data on abortions. I entitled the complete speech *I AM CONFUSED:*

Let me first begin by explaining why I am confused. The Word of God, throughout the Bible, tells me that our God is a God of Truth. His Word at Proverbs 30:5 tells us that "every Word of God is pure". And the scriptures tells us at 2nd Timothy 3:16 that "ALL SCRIPTURE IS GIVEN BY THE INSPIRATION OF GOD." Yet, in spite of this "purity" and the "inspired" nature of the Word of God, daily I see and hear Christians doing and saying things that has me confused. And I am having difficulty seeing how these things that I hear and see square with the Word of God as I know it.

When I was a student in the Seminary, I fell in love with the polls and surveys that were being done to determine what our Christians here in the United States believed about their religion. And I want to look at a recent poll and what it reveals about Christian belief on abortion. As I consider this issue, let me share my personal thoughts and beliefs about abortion.

- When I think about the greatest destructive force in the history of the United States, it's greatest war, and it's greatest moral failure . . . would it surprise you if I told you it would be our practice of legally sanctioned abortions?
- And would it surprise you that I cringe on the inside, and shed tears on the outside thinking about this mindless

slaughter against God's sons and daughters here in the United States?

- I find myself asking the question, "Where is the Church?" Where is the moral outrage of the Christian church?

I find myself thinking back about all of the United States greatest battles, with the greatest loss of American lives, and I find myself grieving because those battles have not and are not being fought on foreign soils in various and sundry lands. But they are being waged right here in our midst, right here in this nation that we call "the home of the brave and the land of the free". I am mindful of the fact that the enemy is not a "them", but us, and I find myself asking the questions:

- How brave must one be to kill an unborn child? And,
- How free are we from the "wages of sin" for our actions? (ROMANS 6:23)

And the "Body of Christ", the Christian Church, has done almost nothing except stand idly by while the most murderous attack in the history of the world is waging in our faces. Some Christians say, "it's not my fault, why should I be held responsible?" Well, the Body of Christ, the church, and it's apathetic response to these violations of Jehovah God's commandments, are responsible because "we" are supposed to be God's very special people. We, as Christians, forget what God's word says about those whom he has chosen. The writer of the book of Hebrews describes us in these words:

"But ye are a chosen generation, a royal
priesthood, a holy nation, a peculiar people; that ye
should shew forth the praises of Him who hath

called you out of darkness into His marvelous
light:" [1st Peter 2:9]

Yes, I am talking about the United States of America's legally sanctioned abortions. I believe that part of the problem is that many men and women in the Body of Christ have no clue about the enormous loss of American lives that have been murdered on the fields of abortion. Maybe that ignorance has led to the Body of Christ's apathy. I don't know.

Let me look through my notes and paint for us several "word pictures" so you will hopefully never forget how great our loss of life has been. We are talking about the loss of future doctors, lawyers, teachers, mechanics, nurses, police officers and firefighters. That is what we have lost in this great assault upon our unborn children. According to my notes, in May of 2010, the prestigious Gallup poll questioned Christians about their beliefs on abortions, and here are the findings:

- 51% of Christians said they were "Pro-life", otherwise they supported the rights of the unborn fetus.
- 42% of Christians said they were "Pro-choice", otherwise they supported the rights of the mother to have the abortion if she wished.

God's Word says in the 6th Commandment – "Thou shall not kill!" He is talking about the killing of mankind. So what is an unborn baby? Yet, 42% of Christians say that they think it is ok to destroy the unborn child. Let's look at a few statistics. For the first one I am going to choose the year of 2004 because all of the data is complete.

Abortion Comparisons - 2004 (totals for the year):

Death by homicide   =   16,137

Death by automobile	=	42,636
Death by abortion	=	1,222,100

That means that on any typical day in the United States in the year 2004, the following occurred:

Daily:

Homicides	=	44
Auto fatalities	=	116
Cancer deaths	=	1,500
Abortions	=	3,348

Since Roe vs. Wade in 1973, more than 50,000,000 legally sanctioned abortions have occurred here in the United States. That is more than the populations of California and Illinois combined, or more than twice the population of Texas. In fact, I discovered through my studies, that each year since Roe vs. Wade, in the United States we kill by abortion more than all the military men and women we have lost in combat in our nation's history. I will list just a few of the major wars so that you can see what I am talking about.

# of US SOLDIERS KILLED

WWI	*= 117,000*
WW11	*= 500,000*
KOREA	*= 54,000*
VIETNAM:	*= 58,000*
TOTAL:	*= 729,000*

After I studies the Roe vs. Wade Supreme Court decision, I was stunned by the use of the 9th Amendment to our Constitution as the foundation of that decision. It is so vague as to be unbelievable, yet it is this amendment that is bringing the United States to its knees. It came about because of all of the in-fighting between the dominant political parties of that time, which was called the "Federalists", and it's opposition.   And it was a compromise. Does that sound familiar?

- U.S. Constitution was ratified in 1787
- 9TH Amendment was ratified in 1791

The 9TH Amendment reads: *"THE ENUMERATION IN THE CONSTITUTION, OF CERTAIN RIGHTS, SHALL NOT BE CONSTRUED TO <u>DENY</u> OR <u>DISPARAGE</u> OTHERS RETAINED BY THE PEOPLE."*

As I close, I am reminded of the fact that this 9th Amendment, who many legal scholars have not been able to make sense of, including at least one Supreme Court Justice, was a "ticking time bomb", embedded by old Satan himself, into our legal system where it lie dormant for 182 years (1791 – 1973) before exploding and creating this abortion fiasco.

REFERENCE
MY TEN FAVORITE SERMONS

As you continue reading, there are a series of documents to this letter which are very important to me. It will give you some ideas into "What I Believe," and "How I Feel," about my God and what He requires of each of us.

I have selected some of my favorite Sermons to share with you. When I was a student at ITGW Theological Seminary I had to take a class on a subject called "Homiletics," which was the art of preparing to preach a sermon. The Sermons that we studied fell into three types. Since we may some future "preachers" out there, I will summarize them for you.

• Expository Sermons – In this type of sermon you take a scriptural passage from which you develop your theme and main points. You may use other scriptures to illustrate or explain.

• Textual Sermons – This type of sermon usually develops a single verse of scripture. The theme and main points must come directly from this single verse, even though other minor points may be made by referring to other verses. NOTE: This is my least favorite method of sermon preparation and presentation.

• Topical Sermons – My favorite type. You take a subject or topic and develop your theme by using the entire Bible.

When you read my sermons you will note that I like to embed the scriptures that I refer to so that they are always there in front of me when I am preaching. I also write my sermons out in full "Manuscript" form so that if anyone wants a copy for further study, I can provide them with one. I hope you enjoy *TEN SERMONS BY AN OLD COUNTRY PREACHER.*

Mount Tabor Baptist Church

NO CROSS, NO CROWN!

"Then Jesus said unto His disciples, if any man will come after Me, let him deny himself, and take up his cross, and follow Me. For whosoever will save his life shall lose it: and whosoever will lose his life for My sake shall find it. For what is a man profited, if he shall gain the whole world, and lose his own soul? Or what shall a man give in exchange for his soul?"
[Matthew 16:24-26]

"Fear none of those things which thou shall suffer: behold the devil shall cast some of you into prison, that ye may be tried; and ye shall have tribulation ten days: Be thou faithful unto death, and I will give thee a Crown of Life." [Revelation 2:10 {last portion}]

The title of this sermon is that if we carry no cross for Jesus, we will wear no crown of life. Otherwise, No Cross, No Crown! In this passage in Matthew, Jesus is teaching his disciples about what will be required of those of us who are to share the rewards of the Kingdom of Heaven with him and his Father.

- He told them that if they wanted to follow him, Christ, they would have to deny themselves, take up their crosses and follow him.
- Then, in the book of Revelations, he told the Apostle John to write the congregation in Smyrna. This was a congregation that was trying to be faithful and was undergoing some persecution. Jesus told John to tell them to just hand in there and not let old Satan the Devil overwhelm them. Jesus said, tell them that if they are faithful unto death, that I would give them a "CROWN OF LIFE".

That is the word that I would like to share with Christians today. If we wish to be disciples of JESUS CHRIST we must deny ourselves, take up our cross and follow him!

- Jesus wants us to stop focusing on the "ME...ME...ME" in our lives. He wants us to forget what we want. You see, he knows that "that" is Satan's favorite trap for us – getting us focused on ourselves instead.
- He wants us to focus our eyes, our desires, our lives, in fact the totality of our beings on Him! That is want Jesus said the Great Commandment was, Let's consider that for a moment. Look at MATTHEW 22:37:

"Jesus said unto him, Thou shall love the Lord thy God with all thy heart, and with all thy soul, and with all thy mind." [Matthew 22:37]

You see, when we obey that commandment, nothing else can be first in our lives but him. So now we might wish to ask ourselves the question, "What is this cross that Jesus is calling for you and me to take up?" We know that the cross that Jesus died upon was an instrument of a cruel form of death, called crucifixion that was sanctioned by the Roman government. Obviously Jesus knew that he was going to die on that Roman cross at Calvary because he was God, yet before he died, he told his disciples that if they wanted to be his, otherwise share eternity with him and his Father, they must deny themselves, take up "their cross" and follow him in death.

- Jesus was not talking about us taking up some wooden tree, stake or cross such as he died upon. But crucifixion "was" and "is" a death dealing process.
- So Jesus wanted something to be killed in you and me just like he was going to be killed!
- We know that Jesus has already taken care of the "heavy stuff" for you and me, he's already paid for my sins and your sins on the cross at Calvary. We don't have to die the way that he died, but he wanted something to die in us! There was something in us that Jesus wanted to die so that we could become "his", or in other words, he wanted to negate, or make null and void.

- To eradicate, or to render to no effect the certainty of death to all of us because our sinful nature. After all, doesn't Romans 3:23 tell us: *"For all have sinned and come short of the glory of God.* And doesn't Romans 6:23 tell us:

> *"For the wages of sin is death; but the gift of God is eternal life through Jesus Christ our Lord."*

I believe that it would help us if we thought of Jesus' death at Calvary as just a "portion" of the bigger picture, a "process" that led to our <u>REDEMPTION,</u> and ultimately our <u>SALVATION.</u> I believe that we can think of it as a kind of equation, that while Jesus has done his part, this is not a one-way street. You and I must do ours! In order for us to finish that equation, he wanted you and me to repent and to bring our lives into harmony with God's Word. That meant that we must be willing to suffer sometimes, and if necessary, even to die or give our lives for Him! And I am sad to say, that's a proposition that many of us, who call ourselves Christians, cannot hang with today. But remember, No Cross, No Crown!

You see, just as Jesus was crucified by dying on that old rugged cross at Calvary, Jesus wanted you and me to "crucify", in other words to kill that old sinful and disobedient nature that we have in us, that we inherited from our forefather Adam. It's really just that simple.

How do we do that?? First, my Christian friends, if we are going to carry the cross that Jesus requires of you and Me, we must "give up" this love affair that we have with ourselves, and focus on our relationship with him. When we do that, we can appreciate what Paul was saying in GALATIANS 2:20:

> *"I am crucified with Christ: nevertheless I live; yet not I, but Christ liveth in me."[Galatians 2:20]*

Our question then is, "how can we bear our cross daily?" First there is a simple answer. We need to strive to be like Jesus! (1) He taught us by Word and by Example; and (2) He commands us to be obedient. Let us pause now and consider what these crosses Jesus was talking about symbolizes for you and me. Being a musician, I am mindful of what the songwriter wrote in that song the "Old Rugged Cross". He said that the Cross of Jesus was "the emblem of suffering and shame". So let's remember that, as we consider what Jesus' cross, and ours, symbolizes for us today.

JESUS' Cross symbolizes:	OUR Cross symbolizes:
Suffering, agony, & death???	*Suffering, agony & death*
Atonement, rebirth & eternal life	*Repentance, rebirth & eternal life*

Jesus died on the cross because the cost was too high for you and me to bear. No one else could pay the price of mankind's sins. Sin was brought into the world by the First Adam, so only Jesus, the Last Adam referred by Paul in 1 Corinthians 15:45 could pay for those sins. So he paid so that you and I could escape the wages of sin and come into the household of God. But remember, No Cross, No Crown!

Now, let's look at some examples of how we can carry our cross for Jesus daily. I will just mention several examples so that you can follow my reasoning.

(1)   WE NEED TO TAKE UP THE CROSS OF OBEDIENCE: (Jesus Said) *"I CAME TO DO THE WILL OF MY FATHER WHO SENT ME". John 14:15 [IF YOU LOVE ME, YOU WILL OBEY MY COMMANDMENTS}. [Note: See John 15:9] Comment: The sole and whole duty of man is to obey God!!*

IF WE ARE OBEDIENT WE WILL:

Mark 12:31   "Love God with our total being"

Luke 6:27   "Love your enemies/Those who hate you"

Galatians 6:2   "Bear ye one another's burdens"

Malachi 3:10   "Bring ye all the tithes into the storehouse"

NOTE: Incidentally. Jesus knew that some of us could never bring ourselves to give God's money back to Him. That is why He taught His disciples In Matthew 6:24 that no man could serve two masters. He went on to say that you cannot serve God & Money. YOU HAVE TO MAKE A CHOICE! In Malachi verse 9: Disobedience = Curse, in verse 10 obedience=Blessing.

(2)   <u>WE NEED TO TAKE UP THE CROSS OF LOVE</u> (Jesus set the example) {AGAPE} A BENEVOLENT, SELFLESS KIND OF LOVE!!

(3)   <u>WE NEED TO TAKE UP THE CROSS OF HUMILITY</u> (Jesus set the example)

> *"He riseth from supper, and laid aside His garments; and took a towel and girded Himself. After that He poured water into a basin, and began to wash the disciples' feet, and to wipe them with the towel wherewith He was girded."*
> *[John 13:4-5]*

(4)   <u>WE NEED TO TAKE UP THE CROSS OF SERVICE</u>

Jesus set the example:

(1) Feed the hungry

(2) Soothe those in morning {also saving lost souls}

(3) Luke 10:2 {Harvest is great/Laborers are few}

(4) Matthew 28:19-20 Go teach all nations!!

(5)   <u>WE NEED TO TAKE UP THE CROSS OF SELF-DENIAL</u>
{Matthew 16:24: "If you want to follow me, put aside your selfish ambitions."}

157

{Luke 9:23: "Put aside your selfish ambitions, and take up your cross &follow me."}

FINALLY, SINCE CHRIST SUFFERED FOR US,

(6) <u>WE MUST TAKE UP THE CROSS OF SUFFERING FOR CHRIST</u>

"For unto you it is given in the behalf of Christ, not only to believe on Him, but also to "SUFFER" for His sake;" [Philippians 1:29]

As I close, these are just a few of the examples of taking up on cross daily and following Jesus. We all know what God wants us to do, but many times we simply allow ourselves to "get in the way" of our salvation. But God's Word tells us that one day there is going to be a Judgment Day when all of us must appear before the Judgment Seat of Christ. And what you did for "self" will not matter. The only thing that will matter is if we have brought our lives in harmony with the Word of God. Our "personal interpretations" of God's Word will not matter they are not in harmony with his Word. You see, God's Word is clear! It will not be about what we "think" but how obedient we are to what God "meant". Paul said at 2nd Corinthians 5:10 that we will be judged on what we have "DONE:!

"For we must all appear before the judgment seat of Christ; that everyone may receive the things done in his body, according to that he has done, whether it be good or bad."[2 Corinthians 5:10]

NOTE: Compare that with what John saw in Revelations 20:12: (last part)

"...And the dead were judged out of those things which were written in the books, according to their works." [Revelation 20:12]

So, if you and I carry our crosses in our daily walk with Christ, there will be no surprises for us on that Judgment Day. Jesus was in agony, he was hurting as he faced the suffering on the Cross, but he was thinking about you and me and he WANTED to pay the price that he knew you and I could not pay. He WANTED to pay so that we could be a part of His family. And if we are "His", there will be many pains incurred as we continue to sojourn on this earth and make the choice to follow Jesus and obey him completely.

Let me close by naming just a few of the pains we can expect to bear:

- The <u>PAIN</u> of rejection by those we love, who no longer understands US
- There is the <u>PAIN</u> of giving up our forbidden relationships
- And oh yes, loving someone who hates you ain't easy!

Finally, Jesus told John that we need to be faithful unto death. We can't just walk "a piece of the way" with Christ. He tells us to take up our crosses "daily". He is asking us to go all the way!

AMEN

CHRIST IS ALL WE NEED!

"Be it known unto you all, and to all the people of
Israel, that by the name of Jesus Christ of Nazareth,
whom ye crucified, whom God raised from the dead,
even by Him doth this man stand here before you
whole. This is the stone which was set at nought of you
builders, which is become the head of the corner.
Neither is there salvation in any other: for there is none
other name under heaven given among men, whereby
we must be saved." [Acts 4:10-12]

Jesus told Thomas: "...I am the way, the truth, and
the life. No one comes to the Father except through
Me." {John 14:6}

It was almost five hundred years ago when a young Catholic Priest by the name of "<u>MARTIN LUTHER</u>" nailed his 95 "Thesis" or propositions for reform, to the front door of the Church in Wittenburg Germany. And today when we look back in history we can see that all of our Protestant Church denominations can be traced back to that one single incident, which was called the "<u>European Reformation</u>". You see, the Medieval Church had simply strayed away from the teachings of Biblical Scriptures and we won't even try to share with you the horrible things that were going on in the Catholic Churches of that era.

But thanks be to God that he was raising up some young men, such as young Martin Luther, who after being taught the truth of God's Word in the Universities and Seminaries, felt that the Church needed to get back to living the Word of God. So this protest, this cry for change, was basically a cry for God's Church to return to obeying the Word of God! As the European Churches began to turn back to God's Word as the "truth" in their lives, among other things, they began to create a series of slogans in which to use as points of focus in their teachings. Since my sermon text this morning will be coming from one of these slogans, let me list the five most important ones so that you can see the direction that these "reformers" were headed.

(1) *"Sola Scriptura"* - The Bible is the final authority in FAITH and LIFE, that <u>Scripture alone</u>, as opposed to church doctrine/tradition or the authority of official clerics in the church.

(2) *"Sola Fide"* - We are justified by <u>Faith alone</u>, not Faith and Works, not faith plus works. We are not justified by works, but we receive that justification by faith alone (Sola Fide).

(3) *""Sola Gratia"* - We are saved by God's Grace to us. By His <u>Grace alone</u>, and not because of anything we have done, or have deserved.

(4) *"Sola Christo"* - We are saved through the person and work of Jesus Christ alone; not Christ plus anything! But by <u>Christ alone</u>.

(5) *"Soli Deo Gloria"* All things are to be done to God's glory.

So our message this morning will be from the fourth slogan "Sola Christo", Otherwise, Christ is all that we need!"

It is sad commentary today that these five truths, that were under attack in the early Church, are still under attack today in our Churches, in our Seminaries, in our Christian pulpits, as well as in our pews!

As I have sat in our Churches these past twenty plus years, I have come to believe that if we are to change that reality, our Churches need to make some drastic changes in several significant areas. Particularly, this must occur in the areas of teaching of God's Word in a manner sufficient for us to "<u>UNDERSTAND</u>" it and

"KNOW" it. In other words, Christian leaders and teachers need to develop in us a body of knowledge that creates within us a system which promotes "Faith in the Word of God!" Many Churches today are so hung up on their traditions. Church will ignore the truth of God's Word so the members are not offended. And instead of "shepherds" who teach the Word of God unadulterated, many of our Churches are lead by politicians who take great efforts to keep their members happy by not treading upon their lifestyles and by not teaching us God's limits that he has placed on his children. So we are left wallowing in the ignorance of God's word. I want to show you why this is so. Turn your Bible to 2nd Timothy 4:2 – 4. I am going to read it from a modern day translation for clarity.

(Paul- Teaching Timothy how to Pastor)

"Preach the Word of God. Be persistent, whether the time is favorable or not. Patiently Correct, Rebuke, and Encourage your people with good teaching. (3) For a time is coming when people will no longer listen to right teaching. They will follow their own desires and will look for teachers who will tell them whatever they want to hear. (4)They will reject the truth and follow strange myths." [2 Timothy 4:2-4]

If we are to be God fearing Christians, we need to take seriously the truth of God's Word and walk in obedience before him.

Let me get back on track. One the one hand, my sermon topic is about "Christ alone", and I am getting excited talking about our need to believe the Word of God. Maybe I should have preached *"Sola Scriptura"* first!

In our scripture from the book of Acts, the Apostle Peter, who was filled with the Holy Spirit, confronted the rulers and elders of the Jews because the Jewish leaders were critical, or maybe just curious, of the fact that the apostles had healed a sick man. The Jewish leaders wanted to know "how" and by what power was it done. Peter let them know that it was done by the power of the name of Jesus! He went on to say, "This is the Christ that you have rejected and crucified!   This is our Lord and Savior . . . there is no other name under the heavens by which we can be saved!" This is a powerful truth that many people during Old Testament times just could not get it.   Sadly, many people who call themselves Christians still have the same questions today. I know that many people have not been exposed to some of the things that are being said about the personage and work of Jesus today that they simply don't believe. There are people who call themselves Christians who question whether of not Jesus Christ is the only way of Salvation. They don't believe John 14:6. They believe that whatever your religion, you will be saved!

"And Jesus said unto him, I am the way, the truth, and the life: No man comes unto the Father, but by Me." [John14:6]

A minister was recently overheard to say "What is the big deal about Jesus? Well, what does the Scripture say about this "Big Deal" called Jesus? The Bible tells us that Jesus Christ alone should be the object of our faith. And Matthew 11:27, 28 lets us know that we must put our trust in Christ alone for our salvation! This is what Peter was talking about when he said, "There is salvation in no one else, for there is no other name under the heaven that has been given among men by which we must be saved!" That is so different from what you can hear in many of the modern day churches. We hear such stuff as:

- All roads leads to Heaven
- There are many ways of knowing God…And all are equally valid!
- There are many religions that teach truth (Islam/Hindu/Buddest, etc)

Yet, God's Word is so clear. It says, "There is only one way, one road to salvation" and that is through Jesus Christ! Yet if we teach God's Word, as he has presented it to us, we may be exposed to all kinds of criticisms. Yes, I have already had that happen to me, being accused of being "intolerant" and accused of being insensitive to others. One fellow said to me, "How dare you Christians say that members of other religions will not be saved. We have a right to determine what is right for us. If we are comfortable with our lifestyles, how dare you say we will not be saved, even if we don't believe in Jesus Christ!" That's why I have not heard any Pastors in these back woods, where I serve, preaching against such things as:

- HOMOSEXUALITY
- SAME SEX MARRIAGE
- ABORTION
- PORNOGRAPHY...AND
- SEXUAL IMORALITY

Yes, we teach about going to heaven, but we act like Hell doesn't exist. Surely, if there is a heaven that the Bible tells us to seek, by being obedient to the Word of God, then there is a hell that God's Word teaches us is the destiny of those of us who are disobedient to the Word of God. Yes, God's Word is very clear on such matters. Romans 6:23 summarizes that reality in no uncertain terms, it says:

> *"For the wages of sin is death; but the gift of God*
> *is eternal life through Jesus Christ our Lord."*
> *[Romans 6:23]*

And Jesus tells us all that we have to do to gain this eternal life with him and his Father. Look at John 14:15:

> *"If you love Me, keep My commandments."*
> *[John 14:15]*

Regrettably, many of us who call ourselves Christians do not want to obey the Word of God, but instead want to follow their own agendas and not God's commands for our lives. And some kind of way we have to make ourselves feel like we are walking in harmony with God's Word. I call that "walking in between the rain drops" and trying not to get wet. I think maybe we need to stop sometimes and just consider why Christ died for us and why, contrary to what many believe, he is the only way, Christ is all that we need! You see the very person and work of Jesus Christ argues against the idea that there are many ways to bring ourselves into fellowship with God. Jesus' death on that redemptive cross at Calvary rules out any other options. At least the apostles were very clear and emphatic about this fact, and early Christians and even others got themselves in trouble from time to time by ignoring this.

There is a story from medieval times that I want to share with you:

> When the Emperor *"SEVERUS"* ascended to the Roman throne around 305 A. D., the Romans served many Gods. So Severus thought he would do the Christians, who were Roman captives, a favor by adding Jesus to the list of Gods he would serve. Severus thought the Christians would be pleased that he was willing to serve their God also. But he was stunned when the Christians rejected that idea, claiming that Christ and Christ alone was worthy to be worshipped because he was the only way to salvation.

All of us who trust in Jesus, the Bible says, whether we be Jew or Greek, slave or free, male or female, trusting in Christ and obeying Him, will cover our sins and bring us into fellowship with the living Almighty God, Jehovah!

As I prepare to close, I want to ask you and I some questions for consideration:

- DO WE WANT TO GIVE THE "TOTALITY" OF OUR BEINGS TO CHRIST AND TO BRING OUR LIVES INTO SUBJECTION TO HIM?
- DO WE BELIEVE THAT JESUS SACRIFICED HIS LIFE HERE ON EARTH FOR YOU AND I? OTHERWISE...
- DO WE BELIEVE THAT HE HUNG...BLED...AND DIED ON THAT CROSS AT CALVARY?
- DO WE BELIEVE THAT SALVATION IS A FREE GIFT THAT COST US ABSOLUTELY NOTHING?

LOOK AT ROMANS 12:1 - THAT LET'S US KNOW WE MUST SACRIFICE OURSELVES TO HIM!!

> *"I beseech you therefore brethren, by the mercies*
> *of God, that ye present your bodies a living sacrifice,*
> *holy, acceptable unto God, which is your reasonable*
> *service."[Romans 12:1]*

It is only reasonable that you and I bring our lives unto subjection and walk in obedience and humility before Christ, our Savior and our Lord.

I close now by saying that God wants us to be a living sacrifice. That means that when we accept Christ as our personal Savior, we choose to obey him over our own will and our own desires. We no longer seek to fill our lives with early pleasures. Instead, we seek to serve Jehovah God in all of our ways. This is not too much for Jesus to ask of us because he gave his life for you and me as "Son of Man", with unspeakable agony, so that you and I could be free from the wages of our sins, which Romans 6:23 tells us is death!

AMEN

EVERYTHING MUST CHANGE

"Therefore if any man be in Christ, he is a new creature: Old things are passed away; behold, all things are become new." [2nd Corinthians 5:17]

"Don't copy the behavior and customs of this world, but let God transform you into a new person by changing the way you think. Then you will know what God wants you to do, and you will know how good and pleasing and perfect His will really is."
[Romans 12:2 NLT]

This sermon, for me, is somewhat of a personal testimony concerning my walk, or failure to walk with Christ, after I claimed him as my Lord and Savior. I am continually amazed at what has transpired in my life in the past several years. You see, I had been "Masquerading" as a "Born Again" Christian for years. And even though I had learned to "talk the talk", I still basically continued along the same foot paths of DISOBEDIENCE and WICKEDNESS that I had trod before. Well, the masquerade is over. I now realize that I had walked in disobedience before this God that I claimed as my own!

I learned very quickly how to hide the true nature of my walk from my so-called fellow Christians. But, that was very easy to do, because many of them walked along the same pathways that I walked. You see, we continued to "DO AS" and "BE AS" we were before our supposed rebirth, or conversion, and that is clearly at odds with God's Word! God's Word tells us that when we are reborn as Christians, we should no longer <u>act</u>, <u>feel</u> or <u>think</u> the same way again. 2 Corinthians teaches us that we are new creatures and that all of the former things in our old "fleshly ways" should have passed away! We might not dress any different, we might not change the car we drive or even our hairstyle, but we should have a new purpose for living. Let's look at 2 Corinthians 5:15:

> *"And that He died for all, that they which live*
> *should not henceforth live unto themselves, but unto*
> *Him which died for them, and rose again."[II*
> *Corinthians 5:15]*

2 Corinthians 5:15 says that we should have stopped living for ourselves and began to live for Christ. Otherwise, it tells us that our focus should change from what "we want" to what our Lord and Savior Jesus Christ wants for our lives. You see, we need to stop viewing our lives through the UNFOCUSED and CLOUDY lens of our old fleshly desires and instead we need to begin to view our lives through the crystal clear leans of God's perspective for us.

Making this change was not easy for me. In fact, it is easier said than done. Particularly when we have lived a lifetime of being what is the word "ethno-centric", or self-centered. I know that it has been very difficult for me to change from being "me-centered" to "Christ-centered". Regrettably, I am still not all the way there. But that is the goal that I continually strive to achieve. It is fairly easy to do a decent job of changing on the outside, but it is the inside of us that really matters! And if we are not very careful, we will find ourselves continuing to think those same old WICKED, INSIDEOUS, and LASCIVIOUS thoughts that we had before we were baptized.

I was sitting around the house one day thinking about my walk with God and I finally figured it out. I had widely missed the mark that the Apostle Paul had talked about in Philippians 3:14. Let us turn there for a moment:

> *"I pressed towards the mark for the prize of the*
> *high calling of God in Christ Jesus."*

[Philippians 3:14]

If the prize that I was striving for was an eternal life in heaven (with "MY" Jesus Christ), and that is what we Christians look forward to, then I had blown it! As I thought about my life up to that point, I realized that I could summarize it in the following words: *I wanted to go to Heaven...But I didn't want to die. In other words...I wanted to hang on to my old sinful nature...and at the same time "claim" that I had been crucified with Christ, as Paul wrote in Galatians 2:20...I call that" Trying to walk between the rain drops.*

> *"I am crucified with Christ: nevertheless I live; yet, not I, but Christ liveth in me: and the life which I now live in the flesh I live by the faith of the Son of God who loved me, and gave Himself for me." [Galatians 2:20]*

I said that I loved the Lord, but I didn't want to obey Him. Jesus said in John 14:15 that if we loved Him we would keep His commandments.

1. I didn't want to love my enemies
2. I didn't want to turn the other cheek
3. I didn't want to <u>forgive</u> sometimes
4. I didn't want to give a significant portion of my income back to God (The Giver)

You see, God had richly blessed me, in aspects of my life, and I didn't want to accept Jesus' Words at Luke 12:48 when he spoke of what is required of us. Let's turn there, and I am going to read from my new Living Translation, the last half of that verse.

> *"...Much is required from the person to whom much is given; Much more is required from the person to whom much more is given." [Luke 12:48] NLT*

I said that I wanted to follow Christ, but I didn't want to carry my Cross. That was a burden that would be oft-times painful &

inconvenient, and I didn't want the <u>inconvenience</u> or the <u>pain</u>! And finally I could not accept the fact that "if I am to be <u>HIS</u>, then I can no longer be <u>MINE</u>. You see, it's kind of hard for us to accept the fact that Jesus purchased us, when he died on the Cross. The Apostle Paul said it like this in 1 Corinthians 6:19-20. Let's look at that scriptural passage:

> *"What? Know ye not that your body is the temple of the Holy Ghost which is in you, which ye have of God, and ye are not your own? For ye are bought with a price: therefore glorify God in your body, and in your spirit which are God's." [I Corinthians 6:19-20]*

I was thinking that in the book of Revelations, Jesus told John about people such as myself when he told John to write a message and send it to the angel at the Church at Laodicea. You see, such as myself, they liked to "walk between the raindrops". Turn your Bibles to Revelations 3:14-16 and see what Jesus had to say about them.

> *"And unto the angel of the church of the Laodiceans write: These things saith the Amen, the faithful and true witness, the beginning of the creation of God; I know thy works, that thy art neither cold nor hot: I would thou wert cold or hot. So then because thou art lukewarm, and neither cold nor hot, I will spue thee out of my mouth. [Revelation 3:14-16]*

You see, in God's eyesight, we either "<u>IS</u>" or we "<u>AIN'T</u>". We are either "<u>His</u>" or we are not. Let me say it like this. If we continue to try to live with one foot in God's way, and one foot in ours, God says that he will spit or vomit us out of his mouth! Otherwise, he will reject us. We have to be willing to change if we choose to follow Jesus Christ!

When I was a young man living in Kansas City, I used to love hanging out in the nightclubs where there was good music, there was a song that I loved very much. The name of it was "Everything Must Change". I no longer remember the words, but one of the lines went something like this:

"EVERYTHING MUST CHANGE. THE YOUNG BECOME THE OLD AND MYSTERIES DO UNFOLD AND THAT'S THE WAY LIFE IS…EVERYTHING MUST CHANGE."

That is what the Apostle Paul is speaking of in 2 Corinthians and in the book of Romans. When we accept Jesus Christ as our Lord and Savior, when we accept his redemptive death on the cross at Calvary and we repent of our sins, we must change.

My mama would say, we can't walk the way we used to walk. We belong to Christ now. Psalm 1 lets us know that we should delight in walking in God's way. We can't talk the way we used to talk. Our minds should no longer harbor evil, vile, and profane thoughts which are manifested via the utterances of curses and profanities of our mouths. We should no longer speak disparagingly and maliciously about one another.

"THE YOUNG BECOMES THE OLD:" We need to put the silly, juvenile and childlike behavior or immature Christians behind us. Otherwise, we need to grow up in Christ. I like the way that Paul said it in his dissertation on love in 1 Corinthians 13.

"When I was a child, I spoke as a child, I understood as a child, I thought as a child: But when I became a man…I put away childish things."
[1ST Corinthians 13:11]

As we continue on this Christian walk of ours, all of us GROW OLDER. But many of us fail to GROW UP in Christ. Otherwise, we fail to attain Christian maturity and we cannot achieve this until we do three things:

(1) We must come into an <u>UNDERSTANDING</u> of God's Word. We do that by continually studying his word. One of the major short-coming of many "serious" Christians is that they don't take time to study God's Word. Paul wrote to young Timothy and told him how important the study of God's Word was. Look at 2ND Timothy 2:15, AND 2ND Timothy 3:16.

> *"Study to shew thyself approved unto God, a workman that need not be ashamed, rightly dividing the Word of truth. [2ND Timothy 2:15]*

> *"All scripture is given by inspiration of God, and is profitable for doctrine, for reproof, for correction, for instruction in righteousness:" [2ND Timothy 3:16]*

How important is it to know God's Word? Let me just give you one modern day example of Christians not knowing God's Word. In California there is a large Christian marketing research firm headed up by a fellow by the name of George Barna. It is called the Barna Research Group, Ltd. Now this company specializes in conducting primary research for Christian ministries and non-profit organizations. In a series of surveys conducted during the 90s, they conducted a series of surveys among Christians to assess their beliefs about the Word of God. Let me share several of the questions with you, and the Christian responses. When this group was asked what they believed about Jesus:

- 35% said that sometimes Jesus made mistakes
- 29% said that Jesus was human and committed sins like everyone else!

Well, what does God's Word say?

> *"For He hath made Him to be sin for us, who knew no sin; that we might be made the righteousness of God in Him." [2nd Corinthians 5:21]*

When asked about the existence of Satan, or the devil, fifty-five percent said Satan the Devil was not a living thing, but was just a "symbol" of evil.

> *"And the great dragon was cast out, that old serpent, called the Devil and Satan, which deceiveth the whole world: he was cast out into the earth, and his angels were cast out with him." [Rev. 12:9]*

> *"And the devil that deceived them was cast into the lake of fire and brimstone, where the beast and the false prophet are, and shall be tormented day and night forever and ever." [Rev. 20:10]*

When asked about the Bible and religious teachings, fifty-seven percent said that all religious faiths teach equally valid truths.

When asked about their views on salvation, forty-five percent believed that if a person is generally good, or does enough good things during life, "that" person will earn a place in heaven. Forty percent believed that all good people, whether or not they consider Jesus Christ to be their Savior, will live in heaven after they die on earth.

(2) We must seek to know and accept God's Ways. Moses prayed . . .

> *"Now therefore I pray Thee, if I have found grace in Thy sight, shew me now Thou way, that I may know Thee. That I may find grace in Thy sight:..."*
> *[Exodus 33:13]*

David said...

> *"The meek will He guide in judgment: and the meek will He teach His way." [Psalm 25:9]*

(3) We must OBEY God's Will . . .

The words of the song said that "MYSTERIES DO UNFOLD." Do you think that God's mysteries have been unfolded to those Christian folk who:

- Believe that Jesus walked the earth as a sinner?
- Believe that Satan does not exist...but is simply a Symbol of evil?

Not hardly! I ask the question then, how can we have faith in God that we know very little, or nothing about? Sadly, that used to be my dilemma. I thank God that is no longer true. As I close, I ask the question, What about you?

AMEN

BLACKS IN THE BIBLE

*(24) "God that made the world and all things
therein,...", (26) "And hath made of one blood all
nations of men for to dwell on all the face of the earth,"
[Acts 17:24 & 26]*

During the month of February, that we designate as Black History Month, I want to spend a few moments talking about the history of blacks in the Bible. I will not be able to treat this subject in great detail. In fact, I will only deal with a few of the blacks in the Old Testament. And maybe for the next few years, if I am still around, I may just preach this kind of sermon each Black History Month, to add to our body of knowledge.

I wanted, during this Black History Month to provide us with some food for thought. At least on a couple of points, and these points are:

(1)   The origin of black people in the Bible
(2)   What the biblical record has to say about these black folks
(3)   How men who called themselves believers, both abroad as well as here in the United States of America, have used their understanding of biblical history to justify the enslavement of our forefathers, and
(4)   The fact that most black people know little or nothing about our black heritage in the Bible! <u>BECAUSE THEY HAVE NOT BEEN TAUGHT!!</u>

Before I begin, I want you to also make a special note of the Scriptures in "Acts 17" that I selected as the sermon's foundational Scriptures. I did that because I wanted to "highlight", I wanted to "emphasize" the "unity" of God's favorite creation, Man, and I wanted to highlight the fact that we all come from a common bloodline. We all are descendants of one couple, Adam and Eve. In fact, Genesis 3:12 says:

> *"And Adam called his wife's name Eve; because she was the mother of all living."[Genesis 3:20]*

NOTE: We may better appreciate Eve's name if we looked at the Hebrew word that we translate into the English language as Eve. The Hebrew word is *"CHAV-VAH", which means "LIFE GIVER."*

Actually, if we think about it, we can be even more precise than that we all have to be descendants of the survivors of the great flood. We are all descendants of Noah! Now, if I may, I want to take the "paint brush" of my mind and spend a few moments painting a brief sketch of the presence of black people and their roles and their status during the beginning of biblical times.

In order to do that, I think that I would have to begin by sharing some historical facts that have led many to believe that there were no blacks of note during biblical times. Or, in fact, they were cursed and were only good for use as slaves. Nothing can be further from the truth!

I want you to understand and "genesis" or the beginning of these "mythical" beliefs and I certainly plan to dispel those myths. I want you to see that black people are very prevalent in the Word of God. I want you to see that they were "<u>present</u>". I want you to see that they were "<u>prominent</u>", and I want you to see that they were "<u>powerful</u>". You see our forefathers have been heavily <u>abused,</u> <u>burdened</u> and <u>oppressed</u> by the writings of ancient historians, ethnologists and Biblical commentators during the past centuries, and even up until today, trying to "explain away" the origin of black people.

Of course, since we are here, they cannot say that we don't exist. So they have used their poisoned minds, stepped in and shaped by their racial prejudices, and some used these convoluted versions of our origins to provide a "Biblical justification" for the enslavement, and the subjugation of black people. I will comment on some of that before I finish.

Let me begin by turning to the 10th chapter of the book of Genesis. We find there what we normally refer to as the "Table of Nations". This tells you about the generations of the sons of Noah and their off-springs after the flood. That was the beginnings of the various nations. Now God, in his infinite wisdom, had decided that he wanted the people of the earth nations to be identified by different "skin colors" and physical characteristics. So he placed different genes in each of Noah's three sons. The names of Noah's three sons were:

- SHEM - WHO BECAME THE FATHER OF THE "SHEMATIC" AND "MONGOLOID" RACES...(THE YELLOW AND TAN RACES)
- HAM - WHO BECAME THE FATHER OF THE "NEGROID" OR BLACK AND TAN RACES, AND
- JAPETH - WHO BECAME THE FATHER OF THE "CAUCASIAN" OR WHITE RACES.

In that 10th chapter of Genesis, I want to take a look at the descendants of Ham. I want to start reading at the 6th verse. (Remember, we are talking about black history). And all blacks are descendants of Ham.

> *"And the sons of Ham; Cush, and Mizraim, and Phut, and Canaan." [Genesis 10:6]*

There is no evidence that Ham was black, but God had placed the black genes in his body. Therefore, all of his four sons, Cush, Mizraim, Phut and Canaan were black! And in some way, all black races and black nations are descendants from Ham's four sons.

Now let's look at the 8th verse of Genesis 10:

> (8) "And Cush begat Nimrod: he began to be a mighty one in the earth. (9) He was a mighty hunter before the Lord: wherefore it is said, even as Nimrod the mighty hunter before the Lord. (10) And the beginning of his kingdom was Babel, and Erech, and Accad, and Calneh, in the land of Shinar.
> [Genesis 10:8-10]

The lineage of Ham's off-springs continues on down through the 20th verse. But I wanted to share that about Cush because he was clearly a black man. In fact, his name literally means, "The Black One". And what about all of these accolades about Cush's son, Nimrod, a black man? The Bible calls him:

- "A MIGHTY ONE IN THE EARTH"
- "A MIGHTY HUNTER BEFORE GOD"
- HE WAS THE BUILDER OF BABEL....WHICH WE NOW CALL BABYLON.
- THE BUILDER OF A CIVILIZATION IN MESOPOTAMIA.

If you look at Geneses 10:10, you will see that Nimrod built the first Kingdom on the earth. So a black man was to be the first one of God's creation to be the King of his own country!

Clearly there existed black people after the flood, and many were prominent people of renown. And there were so many more. Let's look at what went on to occur with Ham's four sons.

We have talked a bit about Cush, he was the founder of the nation of "Ethiopia. WE saw that Ham's second son was named Mizraim. While Cush and his offspring dispersed, Mizraim stayed with his father Ham, who moved to the continent of Africa. After his father dies, Mizraim took over. So what was known then as the "land of Ham" became the land of "Mizraim" in the Hebrew language, which is translated as "Egypt" in the English language. Ham's third son, Phut, founded the country which we now know as Libya. And his fourth son was named Canaan. We ought to all be familiar with the land of the Canaanites, that God told Moses to go and possess.

As I said earlier, I am trying to paint this subject with broad strokes, so I am not dealing with a lot of black individuals. In the Bible, for example, let me pause and share several names of black people in the Bible. We will call this, Did You Know?

- Pharaoh's daughter that founded the baby Moses in the basket, was a black woman! She was a descendant of Mizraim (her name was "Thermuthis")
- We know that Moses 1st wife, ZIPPORAH…was Black
- What about RAHAB the harlot, which was a Great Ancestor of Jesus Christ! Yep, she was a black woman!
- Joseph's wife (Genesis 46:10) was named ASENATH. She was a black woman (Mizraim) She bore him two sons… Manasseh & Ephraim.

Why is this black presence still hidden from us? When we look at stuff like the movie "The Ten Commandments", depicting Moses leading the Jews our of North Africa, you didn't see any black folk except some depicted as "Ethiopians". Yet, at that time there were blacks everywhere in that part of the world.

I don't have time in this brief sermon, but let me share several of the historical views, even of those ancient writers who grudgingly admitted the presence of blacks during this time.

PRE-ADAMITE VIEW:

Writers such as PARACELSUS in 1520, BRUNO in 1591, VANINI in 1619, and PEYRERE in 1665, all wrote that black people were not descendants from ADAM. These writers (all White) argued that Blacks belonged to a race that was created before ADAM. Otherwise, we were not humans, but concluded that we were created to do work "for" humans. As you consider all of this ancient "LUNACY", it didn't just stop there. There is a book written by a world renowned so-called Biblical scholar, ALEXANDER WINCHELL, which was published in 1880. The title of his book was: "Preadamites; or a demonstration of the existence of men before Adam".

CAINITE VIEW:

This view argues that Cain was born white. After he killed his brother, Abel, he was turned black as his punishment. In some of the ancient Jewish writings they say that since Cain's sacrifice before God was unacceptable, the smoke from his sacrifice blew back on him, turned him black and caused all of his children to be born Black. In another Jewish story, a Rabbi writes that God beat Cain with hail until he turned black. Stories vary, but it became a common Euro-American belief that God cursed Cain by turning him Black.

Now let's look at one more of these different views about the origin of the Black Man. I want you to see how silly and insidious these views are. Nonetheless, this kind of thinking has had a serious impact upon our lives. The final view that I will share with you is:

OLD HAMITE VIEW:

This view can be traced back to old Jewish writings, and later adopted by Jewish and Christian interpreters (and I would say especially among the white south in the pre-Civil War period here in the United States). In this view, Ham violated God's supposed prohibition against mating on the Ark. Because he could not resist, he was turned black. Yet another teaching was that Ham and/or Canaan was turned black as a result of Noah's curse in Genesis 9:24-27. In this view, because God cursed Canaan, that the curse was to go on all Canaan's descendants, and the curse was, first, that they would all be turned black, and second, they would be servants to the white races. Again, we see here a blatant attempt by many to interpret the Bible in a way that justifies the institution of black slavery.

I know that a sermon such as this leaves us feeling somewhat nauseated. I also want you to consider what our people, black people, have had to overcome. But thank God he has brought us safely thus far. What you and I must never forget, as we look back at our past, is that God created all of mankind in his image, and has included all members of the human race in the saving work of his son. We can find nowhere in the Word of God that "any people" are outside of the embrace of God's love.

That is all. Hopefully next year we will continue by looking at some more of the black individuals in the Old Testament – people such as the Queen of Sheba. Until then . . .

AMEN

THE SEVEN DEADLY SINS

"For all have sinned and fall short of the glory of God." [Romans 3:23]

"For the wages of sin is death, but the gift of God is eternal life in Christ Jesus our Lord." [Romans 6:23]

This sermon is about sins. Not SIN, but SINS. The Bible is very clear on the "Acts of disobedience" that God calls sins. And we can find these actions listed in many ways and many places throughout the Word of God. In fact, some of them are grouped together in lists (A good example of that is the Ten Commandments). Since there exist a list of sins that are called the "Seven Deadly Sins", I will simply use that as my topic. Seven Deadly Sins. But we will describe and consider many kinds of sins.

I think that first, I need to tell you that there is no "list" in the Bible that list seven sins, calling them the Seven Deadly Sins. But, when I get to that list you will note that they are all listed in the Word of God. But this list of the "Seven Deadly Sins" was created by a Catholic Pope named "Gregory the Great", and he created this list back in the sixth century A.D. But first, you may ask me why are we going to look at all of these descriptions of sin. We know what they are, so why bother?

We are going to take a close look at how sinful behavior is described in God's Word because God's people continue to observe "some" sinful actions, while ignoring others. And when you question some Christians, they fail to note the severity of the punishment for some of the things they do, which God hates. I believe it's because they have not been taught right.

Now let's look at several of the Biblical lists of specific sins in the Word of God. As I have indicated, we all are familiar with The

Ten Commandments, so we will not consider that list, and we will consider the "man-made" list, the one called the Seven Deadly Sins.

The Apostle Paul wrote extensively about sin and its consequences. That is why we used Romans 3:23 and 6:23 as foundation scriptures for this sermon. Paul even provided us with several scriptural passages wherein he gave us a list of behaviors that God did not like. We find one of the Apostle Paul's lists in the first chapter of Romans, beginning at the 28th verse. Let us consider.

> *(28) "And even as they did not like to retain God in their knowledge, God gave them over to a debased mind, to do those things which are not fitting;(29) being filled with all unrighteousness, sexual immorality, wickedness, covetousness, maliciousness; full of envy, murder, strife, deceit, evil-mindedness; they are whisperers, (30) backbiters, haters of God, violent, proud, boasters, inventors of evil things, disobedient to parents,(31) undiscerning, untrustworthy, unloving, unforgiving, unmerciful;(32) who knowing the righteous judgment of God, that those who practice such things are deserving of death, not only do the same but also approve of those who practice them."*
> *[Romans 1:28-32]*

Here is another one of Paul's lists of sinful behaviors. We find this one in the 5th chapter of Galatians:

> *"Now the works of the flesh are evident, which are: adultery, fornication, uncleanness, lewdness, idolatry, sorcery, hatred, contentions, jealousies, outbursts of wrath, selfish ambitions, dissensions, heresies, envy, murders, drunkenness, revelries, and the like; of which I tell you beforehand, just as I also told you in time past, that those who practice will not inherit the Kingdom of God." [Galatians 5:19-21]*

Now let's go look at an Old Testament list of sins (not the Ten Commandments) and see how they are described. Turn your Bibles to Proverbs 6 beginning at verse 16.

> *(16) "There are six things that the Lord hates, yes, seven are an abomination to Him: (17)A proud look, A lying tongue, Hands that shed innocent blood, (18) A heart that devises wicked plans, Feet that are swift in running to evil, (19) a false witness who speak lies, and one who sows discord among brethren."*
> *[Proverbs 6:16-19]*

See how different this list of some of the behavior that God hates is put together. Nonetheless, God's Word is very clear on what he finds to be an "abomination" to him.

Finally, let's look now at the "man-created" list commonly referred to as the "Seven Deadly Sins". As I indicated earlier, each of these sins are referred to in the Word of God, but there is no singular biblical list that contains all of them. We will discuss each one of them individually, and make biblical references to them when necessary. I will also mention a Godly "virtue" which these "sins" are in opposition to.

(1)   <u>PRIDE</u>: (SIN) - (VIRTUE: HUMILITY)

We see this sin listed among Paul's list in Romans 1. Paul says that whoever practices this sin "WILL NOT INHERIT THE KINGDOM OF GOD!" We also see this sin of pride again in the Old Testament list in Proverbs 6. The writer lets us know that pride is something that God hates. Please note that pride is just the opposite of the Godly virtue called "<u>humility</u>" that God wants his children to display.

(2)   <u>GREED</u>: (VIRTUE: GENEROSITY)

We also find the sin of greed (covetousness) found in Paul's list in Romans 1. This is not just about money and material things. The opposite of greed is "generosity". Generosity means more than just giving. It also means letting others get the credit or praise for things without you, and not running around bragging about the credit. It is giving without having "expectations". Greed on the other hand wants to receive more than its fair share.

(3)   ENVY: (VIRTUE: LOVE)

We find envy in both of Paul's lists in Romans 1, as well as Galatians 5. The virtue against which envy sins is "love". Love is patient, love is kind . . . love actively seeks the good of others for their sake. On the other hand, envy resents the good others receive. Envy is almost indistinguishable from "pride" at times. Envy is jealousy!

(4)   ANGER/WRATH: (VIRTUE: KINDNESS)

We find wrath, or anger, in Paul's "works of the flesh" list in Galatians 5. Its opposite virtue is kindness. Kindness means taking the tender approach, with patience and compassion. Anger, on the other hand, is an evil agitation of the soul and manifests itself as a "violent emotion". The difference between anger and wrath is that anger is the "stirring up" of the soul whereas wrath is the "boiling over" of our passions, which results in damaging words or actions. In other words, anger can lead to wrath. Another way to look at this is that anger may begin small and continue growing until it becomes wrath.

(5)   LUST: (VIRTUE: SELF CONTROL)

Lust is the self-destructive drive for pleasure out of proportion to its worth. Otherwise, lust easily becomes an "out of control" drive. Therefore, its opposite virtue is self-control. Remember – a lustful nature is one that forces on immoral or illegitimate pleasures. Self-control prevents our quest for pleasure from killing the soul by "suffocation". On the other hand, legitimate pleasures are controlled in the same way an athlete's muscles are – for maximum efficiency, with no damage.

(6)   GLUTTONY: (VIRTUE: TEMPERANCE)

The appearance of gluttony on this list of the seven deadly sins may come as a shock to some of you. In fact, while we are quick to consider drunkenness as a sin, we almost never consider gluttony in the same light. They are in fact the same kind of sin. Let us look at a scripture or two and see how these two sins are mentioned together.

"And they shall say unto the elders of his city, this, our son is stubborn and rebellious, he will not obey our voice; he is a glutton, and a drunkard."
[Deuteronomy 21:20]

"For the drunkard and the glutton shall come to poverty: and drowsiness shall clothe a man with rags. [Proverbs 23:21]

I believe that this sin of gluttony is one of the major causes of the many illnesses that we struggle with today. I "know" that is certainly true in my case. On the other hand, temperance accepts the "natural" limits of the things we find pleasurable, and preserves God's natural balances in our lives.

(7)   SLOTH (LAZINESS): (VIRTUE: ZEAL)

To be slothful is to be lazy or complacent. Yes, that is a biblical sin. In fact, God's Word has much to say about a slothful man. Let's look at several scriptures concerning slothfulness.

"The way of the slothful man is as an hedge of thorns:…"
[Proverbs 15:19]
"He also that is slothful in his work is brother to him that is a great waster." [Proverbs 18:9]

"A slothful man hideth his hand in his bosom, and will not so much as bring it to his mouth again." [Proverbs 19:24]

"That ye be not slothful, but followers of them who through faith and patience inherit the promises." [Hebrews 6:12]

And if you think God's Word is very unkind to those who are lazy, or slothful, let me show you what God's Word has to say about the lazy ones who fail to provide for their own.

"But If any provide not for his own, and specifically for those of his own house, he has denied the faith, and is worse than an infidel." [1st Timothy 5:8]

Note: That word INFIDEL can better be defined as an UNBELIEVER. On the other hand, the opposite of laziness is Zeal, which is the energetic response of our hearts to God's commands. Slothfulness deadens our spiritual senses so that we become slow to respond to God. Finally, we drift completely into the sleep of complacency.

One of the reasons that I believe that Pope Gregory coined this list of seven sins, and referred to them as being "deadly" is because many people who call themselves "Christians" do not take these sins seriously, especially our young people and the people that they idolize. For example, back in august of 1993, MTV did a special on these seven deadly sins. When they interviewed some of the well known entertainers from the music and television industry, they pretty much all agreed that these were not vices, or sins, in their opinion. And they basically agreed that the list was dumb, that it had no relevance to them. Also, in a recent online poll, people were asked the following question: "Of the seven deadly sins, this ONE is my biggest failing."

THE RESULTS OF THE POLL WERE AS FOLLOWS:

Lust	35%
Anger	18%
Pride	12%
Sloth	10%
Envy	10%
Gluttony	9%
Greed	6%

I hope that each on hearing (reading) this sermon will gain additional insight into how important it is to live our lives in harmony with the Word of God. And I am sure that each one of us can find a practice in our lives listed in this sermon that God is not pleased with. Maybe we don't even know that the practice is not in harmony with the Word of God! That is why God told the Prophet Hosea:

"My people are destroyed for lack of knowledge:"
{Hosea 4:6}

Lets you and me tuck the Word of God away in our hearts and be like the Psalmist: *"But his delight is in the law of the Lord ;and in His law doth he meditate day and night."[Psalm 1:2]*

May God bless those who study his Word.

AMEN

THE PARABLE OF THE SOWER

"And He (JESUS) taught them many things by
parables, and said unto them in His doctrine, behold
there went out a sower to sow: [Mark 4:2-3]

I want you to consider this message that Jesus is sharing with his followers as he is teaching them, as reported in the Gospels.   I have chosen the parable of the seed sower because it symbolizes the different kinds of people that are in the church today!   This "PARABLE OF THE SOWER," is found, not only in the 4th chapter of Mark, but also in the 13th chapter of Matthew, and the 8th chapter of Luke.

Many people will ask, why is it that Jesus loved to speak in Parables. If you will read the parable of the sower in each one of the three Gospels, you will come away with a clear understanding of why Jesus taught that way. Let's take a look at one of the scriptural passages which describes Jesus' reasons.

"Therefore speak I to them in parables: because
they seeing...see not; and hearing...they hear not,
neither do they understand. (14) And in them are
fulfilled the prophecy of Isaiah, which says... 'By
hearing ye shall hear but not understand; and seeing ye
shall see, and shall not perceive:
(Isaiah 6:9)...[Matthew 13:13:14]

Now let's look at this parable verse by verse. The format that I want to use is to read a verse from the parable, and then drop down and read where Jesus explains just what that verse means:

"Hearken; behold there went out a sower to sow."
Mark 4:3

Question: What did the sower sow? Look at verse 14:

"The sower soweth the word." [Mark 4:14]

"And it came to pass, as he sowed, some fell by the wayside, and the fowls of the air came and devoured it up." [Mark 4:4]

Jesus explains: (verse 15), the seed that fell by the wayside represents those who hear the message, only to have Satan come at once and take it away!

"And some fell on stony ground, where it had not much earth; and it immediately it sprang up, because it had no dept of earth: (6) but when the son came up, it was scorched; and because it had no root, it withered away." [Mark 4:5-6]

Jesus explains, (verse 16-17) The seed that fell on rocky soil represents those who hear the message and immediately receive it with joy (17) But since they don't have deep roots, they don't last long. They fall away as soon as they have problems, or, are persecuted for believing God's Word!!

"And some fell among thorns, and the thorns grew up, and choked it, and it yielded no fruit." [Mark 4:7]

Jesus explains: (vs18-19) The seeds that fell among the thorns are others who hear God's Word, (19) but all too quickly the message is crowded out by the worries of this life, the lure of wealth, and the desire of other things, so no fruit is produced in their lives.

"And other fell on good ground, and did yield fruit that sprang up and increased; and brought forth, some thirty, and some sixty, and some an hundred." [Mark 4:8]

Jesus explains: (verse 20) The seeds that fell upon fertile soil represents those who <u>hear</u> and <u>accept</u> the word of God. They are productive Christians and produce a harvest of 30, 60, or even 100 times as much as have been planted!

As we can see by this parable of the seed sower, and since I am one of those called by God to be a seed sower, a sower of the Word of God, I want all to take note of the four different kinds of people that hears the Word of God and how they respond to it. I want you to also note that our response to the Word of God is determined by the nature of our hearts. When we are exposed to the Word of God's truth, we all fall into one of these four categories of listeners. So let me make a few comments about each one. Hopefully you will identify which one you are in, and if you are not, where you're supposed to be. Then that means that you have some work to do, if you are to be a disciple of Jesus Christ.

I also want you to note that only one of these four categories of "HEARERS OF GOD'S WORD" will pass the test of salvation and will be welcomed into the Kingdom of God! This should come as no surprise to anyone. Jesus, while he was teaching his followers at the Sermon on the Mount, let us know that most of the folk that claimed to be "his", that is, "THOSE WHO CALL THEMSELVES CHRISTIANS", would not be with him and his father, enjoying an eternity in heaven!

Let us look again at what Jesus said at Matthew 7:13 – 14:

> *"Enter ye in at the strait gate: for wide is the gate, and broad is the way, that leadeth to, destruction, and many there be which go in there at: (14) because strait is the gate, and narrow is the way, which leadeth unto life, and few that be that find it." [Matthew 7:13-14]*

Let me make some general comments about these four groups of hearers. Here we go:

THE "WAY-SIDERS": (V-4) "And some fell by the Way Side."). This first group is the one that I call the "way siders". They are just there. They go, and they listen. But, as Jesus pointed out they do not <u>perceive</u> or <u>understand</u> the mysteries of the Word of God. They do not come to church to worship God or be affected by anything that they hear. Now, if the Word is placed before them in a manner that is entertaining, they may consider what is said for a brief moment. But very shortly they will have forgotten everything relevant to serving Jehovah God that was said.

I am on occasion confronted with those of my friends, who talk about what a great message the speaker brought, but when you inquire as to the subject, or the focus of the message, or the scriptures used, you find out that they don't remember. Otherwise, they have no clue! You see, they were more impressed or entertained by the speaker's delivery than the Word of God, if there was any! And in my community I have listened to many great speakers, but very few great "teachers"!

THE "STONY GROUNDERS": (V-5) "And some fell on Stony Ground.")

In this second group of hearers, we find a slightly different response. You can just imagine what happens when you sow your seeds among the rocks, without adequate soil your seed may flourish for a moment, but it quickly dies because it has nothing to sustain it! I want to let you know that this class of hearers enjoy, and wan to hear the Word, and they receive it with gladness. But they have a "hardness in their hearts" that fails to allow the Word of God to anchor deeply. So when they encounter the <u>Trials</u> and <u>Tribulations</u> that is sure to come into all of our lives, they quickly fall by the wayside.

At least this second class of hearers gives those of us who are sowers some <u>hope</u> and some <u>joy</u>. But when the initial excitement wears away, or someone is critical of them because they enjoyed the Word of God and reacted to it favorable, they quickly fade away. This is a cause for much sadness among us that sow the Word of God.

THE "THORNY GROUNDERS": (V-7) "And some fell among thorns.")

There is a decided difference of this third category of hearers. From the first two, this group is planted in good soil. Remember, we are talking about the condition of our hearts. The first group of seeds were planted in an inappropriate heart. They reflect those who are actually enemies of God. The second group of seeds were planted in hearts that had been hardened, for whatever reason. The "rocky soil" represents a heart that is not suitable for growing and nurturing the Word of God. But here with the "thorny grounders", we have found some good and deep fertile soil. It is the kind that will grow practically anything.

But with this class of hearers, in spite of the deep and fertile soil, God's Word has some competition. Jesus, in this parable referred to them as thorns in a wheat field. Otherwise, Satan's <u>trash</u> in the midst of God's <u>treasures</u>. We have a lot of this kind of Christians in our churches today.

- THEY HEAR THE WORD OF GOD
- THEY TAKE THIS TRUTH HOME
- THEY STUDY IT
- THEY EVEN MAKE A PROFESSION OF THEIR FAITH IN GOD!
- THEY ATTEND CHURCH AND BIBLE STUDY ON A REGULAR BASIS

- THEY GIVE CONSIDERABLY TO THEIR CHURCH AS WELL AS TO THOSE THAT ARE LESS FORTUNATE.

Doesn't that sound great? It seems that the sower will now finally be successful. But wait, there is a problem with this group. They have **DISTRACTIONS**! They have **RESPONSIBILITIES**, INTERESTS, and PASSIONS and other things that they allow to supplant God's Words and God's requirements. They have no clue as to the implications of what the Word of God at Matthew 22:37 means:

> *"Jesus said unto him, Thou shall love the Lord thy God with all thy heart and with all thy soul, and with all thy mind." [Matthew 22:37]*

It is within the temptations of the "thorny ground" that the evilness of Satan appeals to his victims. It is:

- THE LUST OF THE FLESH
- GREED
- PRIDE
- WEALTH
- HOBBIES

And there are other temptations that the "thorny" Christians permit to push our God back in their agendas, into 2nd place and even 3rd place, in their lives. Oh, they come so close, but Jesus said at Matthew 6:24 that *"NO MAN CAN SERVE TWO MASTERS: FOR EITHER HE WILL HATE THE ONE, AND LOVE THE OTHER; OR ELSE HE WILL HOLD TO THE ONE, AND DESPISE THE OTHER."* Our thorny ground hearers have failed that test!

The Apostle Paul wrote in his letter to the Roman congregation at Chapter 12 verse 2 __*"THAT WE SHOULD NOT BE*

CONFORMED TO THE THINGS AND WAYS OF THE WORLD... BUT...THAT WE SHOULD BE TRANSFORMED...BY CHANGEGING THE WAY WE THINK. It is only then that we can walk in all of the fullness that God has for his people. Sadly, our "thorny ground hearers" have flunked that test also.

THE "GOOD GROUNDERS": (V-8) "And other fell on good ground.")

And now, let us look at the final category of hearers, because these are the ones that passes the test. This is the one that you should spend the rest of our lives in the pursuit of. Jesus said at Luke 8:15 *"HAVE A GOOD AND HONEST HEART...THAT AFTER HEARING GOD'S WORD ...WE WOULD STRIVE TO KEEP IT...AND ALLOW IT TO BRING FORTH ITS FRUIT WITH PATIENCE!!*

Now this "good ground" that these disciples labor in has been made good by the grace of our Lord. Remember, it ain't about "us", it is about "him". Because of our obedient hearts (remember – it is about the condition of our hearts), the Word of God "penetrates" our hearts, and it produces all kinds of Godly things within us. It may be:

- A SUFFICIENCY OF LOVE
- A PASSION OF GIVING TO THOSE IN NEED
- A FERVANT DESIRE TO LEAD OTHERS TO CHRIST
- A DEVOTION TO UNSELFISHLY WORK FOR GOD'S KINGDOM, AND
- A NEED TO BECOME A PRAYERFUL INTERCESSOR FOR OTHERS

Yes, these "hearers" of God, that stand on the "good ground" are those that the Apostle Paul was writing about at Galatians 5:22-23 when he talked about the fruits of the Holy Spirit.

"But the fruit of the Spirit is Love, Joy, Peace, Longsuffering, Gentleness, Goodness, Faith, Meekness and Self-Control!! Against these things there is no law." [Galatians 5:22-23]

As I close, let's you and me, by the grace of God, seek to bring the conditions of our hearts into a heart that God's Word will find "Good Ground".

AMEN

WALKING BETWEEN THE RAINDROPS

Jesus taught at the Sermon on the Mount:

> *"No man can serve two masters: for either he will hate the one, and love the other; or else he will hold to the one, and despise the other. Ye cannot serve GOD and mammon." [Matthew 6:24] {Note: Mammon = wealth}*

There is a reason why man cannot serve God and something else. It is called "SIN." I think that we can better understand the nature of sin when we call it for what it is, and that is disobeying God. The Apostle Paul told the Galatians at 5:16, 17

> *"This I say then, walk in the Spirit, and ye shall not fulfill the lust of the flesh. For the flesh lusteth against the Spirit, and the Spirit against the flesh: these are contrary the one to the other: so that ye cannot do the things that you would. [Galatians 5:16-17]*

What the Apostle Paul is telling us in this scriptural passage is that there is a constant battle going on within us as Jehovah God's sprit comes against our fleshly spirit, in an effort to bring our flesh into harmony with his. Therefore, one of the things that God is calling upon those of us who are called to teach is to teach his truth, and teach it "unadulterated" truths such as:

- Loving God with the totality of our beings
- Loving our fellowman as we love ourselves
- Serving God by giving of ourselves and resources back to Him

The full title of this message is "TRYING TO WALK BETWEEN THE RAINDROPS WITHOUT GETTING WET!!" That may sound humorous, but it is a sad statement of truth today. Our churches are filled with those who call themselves Christians, who call themselves children of God! Even though they try to live in two worlds, they say that the God of Abraham, Isaac and Jacob is their God. But considering some of the things Christians are doing today, it's clear to me that they instead succumb to the desires of their flesh and act like they are their own Gods!

You see, there are many of us that think that we can fulfill the obligations of being God's sons and daughters by simply showing up for church once or twice a week, and then going back out into the world to "do our own thing"! Talking the talk sounds good, but that will not get us into heaven. It's "walking the walk" that counts. That is why the Word of God continues to hammer away at "<u>HYPOCRISY</u>". Look at what Jesus said (Matthew 23:28) and what the Apostle John wrote (1 John 3:18):

> *"Even so ye also outwardly appear righteous unto men, but within ye are full of hypocrisy and iniquity [Matthew 23:28]*

> *"My little children, let us not love in word, neither in tongue; but in DEED and in TRUTH." [1 John 3:18]*

What we see so often today is so many of our fellow Christians trying to walk in two different worlds. I want to show you what the Apostle Paul wrote about the times we are living in, in 2nd Timothy 3, the 1st , 2nd and 5th verses:

> *(1) "You should also know this, Timothy, that in the last days there will be very difficult times. (2) For people will love only themselves and their money. They will be boastful and proud, scoffing at God, disobedient to their parents, and ungrateful. They will consider nothing sacred.... (5) They will act as if they are religious, but they will reject the power that could make them godly..." [2 Timothy 3:1-5] {NLT}*

What about you and me? Where do we stand today? I believe that it is important that we check ourselves from time to time and see how we measure up to God's Word, God's commands, God's laws and God's precepts. Are we really trying to obey God and keep his commandments, or are we just "trying to walk between the raindrops without getting wet?"

We could simply stop after discussing obedience to God's Word because being obedient to God's Word is "CRITICAL" to everything else that e talk about. Jesus, who was God the Son, said in John 14:15

"If you love Me, keep My commandments."
[John 14:15]

Throughout the Old and New Testament Scriptures, God's Word continually reminds us that if we are God's own, we must obey him. Let us look at some of God's requirements for our consideration. We can check ourselves with a few questions that only we can answer for ourselves.

The first set of questions are based on Matthew 22:37:

"Jesus said unto him, Thou shall love the Lord thy God with all thy heart, and with all thy soul, and with all thy mind." [Matthew 22:37]

- Is our walk with Christ of such a nature that we get that command right?

- Do we love God with the "totality of our being", placing him first in ALL aspects of our lives?

- Do we focus our lives on serving and obeying God "before" our family and "before" our jobs, "before" our money and possessions all the time? Or,

- Do we just walk between the rain drops and love, obey and serve God at our convenience, only when we want to?

You know the answer. Our second set of questions come from Luke 6: 27 – 28:

> *"But I say unto you which hear, love your enemies,*
> *do good to them which hate you, Bless them that curse*
> *you, and pray for them that despitefully use you. "*
> *[Luke 6:27-28]*

- Do you love and help those that you don't even particularly care for? Would you give them the shirt off of your back? Would you share your last dollar with them?

- What about those you know that would misuse and abuse you if they got the chance. Would you love them anyway?

- And what about those that you know don't like you. They hate your circumstances. They are envious and jealous of you. Do you love them "beyond a shadow of a doubt?"

- What if you have a conflict with a brother or sister within your fleshly family, or your Christian family? Even if they are the ones that did you wrong. Do you go to them and reconcile your differences? That is what Jesus taught his disciples at the Sermon on the Mount.

I have heard people say that they have forgiven everyone, except maybe a single person that did them wrong many years ago. And they tell me that they know that God understands. That, my Christian friends, is sinning against God's Word, or just trying to "WALK BETWEEN THE RAINDROPS WITHOUT GETTING WET."

Now let's switch gears for a moment. The third question that we will consider comes from what we refer to as the "GREAT

COMMISSION" that Jesus gave to those who are his. But before we go there, let's be reminded of a concern that Jesus had about the "HARVEST" OF SOULS" that he wanted. You see, one of the reasons you and I were created, was so we could be God's "instruments of the harvest". Paul says it this way

> *"For we are labourers together with God:" [1 Corinthians 3:9]*

Jesus said and then commanded his disciples:

> *"Therefore said He unto them, the Harvest truly is great, but the labourers are few: Pray ye therefore unto the Lord of the harvest, that He would send forth labourers unto His harvest." [Luke 10:2]*

> *"Go ye therefore, and teach all nations, baptizing them in the name of the Father, and of the Son, and of the Holy Ghost: Teaching them to observe all things whatsoever I have commanded you: and, lo, I am with you always, even to the end of the world. Amen." [Matthew 28:19-20]*

So, our question today, if you are a Christian is *what have you done or what are you doing about this commandment?*

- Do you set aside a certain amount of time to go out and recruit men and women to come into the Body of Christ?

- Do you work hard at it, are you insistent, dogmatic about this responsibility?

- Do you feel any sense of responsibility for those seats that you see are empty in your congregation?

- God's Word says in 2 Peter 3:9 that he wished all mankind was saved, that none should perish but "repent". As sons and daughters of the Most High God, as co-laborers with Christ, we must work diligently to make this happen.

You know that needs to be done, but is your attitude – let someone that is more qualified do it, or, I have tried but I am not very good at it, so it's not my calling. I don't have the time. EXCUSES!! EXCUSES!

I see many Christians today who seem to believe that the God they serve today is not like the God of the Old Testament. And in spite of all of the examples of how God deals with disobedience, many folk feel safe worshipping Jehovah God, while still ignoring his Word, because it does not "fit" what "we" want to do.

God even sent us his son, Jesus, who was God himself. Who before he went to the Redemptive Cross at Calvary, spent his time teaching his followers of what was to come if they did not live in according to God's Word. And still some kind of way, some of us still feel that neither God the Father, nor God the Son meant what they said! So we continue to live life as we wish.

During these "latter days" God is calling for his children, you and me, to bring our lives into harmony with his Word. We don't have a choice in this matter. Either we are "his" or we are not! And if we are "his" we must obey him. I think back when I was a kid, I wouldn't dare be disobedient to my father because I knew what the consequences would be.

As I close, let me make this observation. Satan, in the form of sin (which is disobedience), has been plaguing God's children since the days of Adam and Eve. Man is born with a sinful nature. That's why God had to send his son to redeem us. But he allows us to make our own decisions. He chose all of us, but we don't have to choose him! Sadly, that is what many people, who call themselves Christians, including me at one time, have done.

When you get a chance I would like for you to read how the Apostle Paul described his struggle with the sin in his life. I'd like you to just read Romans Chapters 7 and 8, beginning with 7:14, and read through the eighth chapter. In this you will clearly see, not only the nature o four individual struggles, but you will see the marvelous solution that God provided for our rescue from an eternal death with Satan (REVELATION 20:10, 15).

AMEN

PATTERNING OUR LOVE AFTER GOD

*"For God so LOVED the world until He gave His
only begotten Son, that whosoever believeth in Him
should not perish, but have everlasting life."
[John 3:16]*

*"But I say unto you, LOVE your enemies, Bless
them that curse you, do good to them that hate you, and
pray for them which despitefully use you, and persecute
you;" [Matthew 5:44]*

Some time ago I was sitting around the house thinking about how good God had been to me. I was thinking about how "rambunctious" I had been in my younger days, how dangerously I had lived, and how most of my friends from that period are deceased. And yet God had spared me for such a time as this.

I thought about the transformation that God's love had created in me when I accepted Christ as my Lord and Savior, and I praised God for not giving up on me. And as I look back over my life, I realized that:

- I HAD BEEN AN <u>EVIL</u> AND <u>VILE</u> MAN AT POINTS...DURING MY LIFETIME, BUT GOD JUST KEPT ON LOVING ME.

- I HAVE BEEN <u>SELFISH</u>, <u>ARROGANT</u>, AND <u>UNCARING</u> AT TIMES, BUT GOD JUST KEPT ON LOVING ME.

I thought about what I "should" have been, and what I "would" have been had it not been for God's love for me. And so I began to search the scriptures on this word we call love and I began to bask in the knowledge of the <u>Caring</u>, <u>Nurturing</u> and <u>Forgiving</u> nature of God's love. From that bit of reflection, I began to think about what we call L-O-V-E in our Christian lives, and I found myself wondering about what do we think God's Word is saying when we read scriptures such as <u>John 3:16</u> (God so loved the world) AND <u>Matthew 5:44</u> (Love thy enemy), and then scriptures such as <u>1 John 4:16.</u>

> *"And we have known and believed the LOVE that*
> *God has for us. God is LOVE, and he who abides in*
> *LOVE abides in God, and God in him."*
> *[1 John 4:16 – NKJ]*

We all have this idea of love in us, and we oftimes express it in many ways. When I was a young man growing up in the 5th ward of Houston, Texas, and feeling a desire to be what we called at that time "hip", I had a need to try to impress the young ladies with my "hip" conversation. And the subject of love seems to have had its "magical sway" upon us young people. So in order to demonstrate my "wiseness", I came up with my own special definition of what love was. If I remember correctly, I think that it went something like this:

"LOVE WAS THE <u>FEELING</u>, THAT YOU <u>FELT</u>, WHEN YOU <u>FELT</u> LIKE YOU NEVER <u>FELT</u> BEFORE."

Well, that sounded pretty impressive to my young mind and sufficed for the moment. But after they had to do an emergency appendectomy on me when I was a teenager, I realized that all of the pain and suffering that I went through, also fit my definition of love. Therefore, my definition of love was neither <u>accurate</u> or <u>adequate</u>. Any, what was not the kind of love that we are reading about in God's Word. So I ask the question, "Are we all on the same page when we talk about the Christian or the Godly love that we read about in God's Word?"

I want us to look at the words in the New Testament that are translated as L-O-V-E. We need to make sure we understand what God's Word is saying when it talks about love. In the New

Testament, the Bible speaks basically, and generally, of two kinds of love. And in the Greek language they are represented by the words "PHILEO," and its derivatives, the word "AGAPE" and its derivatives. Let's first consider the Greek word Phileo, which is the second most common form of the word love in the New Testament, and one which we will see throughout the New Testament.

PHILEO:

This word, and its many derivatives, means to have affection for or fondness of something or someone. This word is kind of similar to what many of us mean when we talk about love.

- I could say that I "phileo" to go hunting. We see an example of this word in Matthew 6:5.

  "And when thou prayest, thou shall not be as the hypocrites: For they PHILEO to pray standing in the synagogues and in the corners of the streets, that they may be seen of men.." [Matthew 6:5]

- I could say that I "philandros" my wife, we see that word in Titus 2:4.

  "That they may teach the young women to be sober, to PHILANDROS their husbands, to PHILANDROS their children..." [Titus 2:4]

We are all familiar with the city of Philadelphia, the City of Brotherly Love they call it. Well, we see the same Greek word, Philadelphia, in Romans 12:10.

  "Be kindly affectioned one to another with PHILADELPHIA..." [Romans 12:10]

And then there is a special "P.H.I.L.E.O" word for the love of money. We see that in 1st Timothy 6:10.

> *"For the PHILARGURIA of money is the root of all evil."*

AGAPE:

This is another Greek word for love. "Agape", it is the most common form of love spoken of in the New Testament and we will spend some time examining this word closely because it is a foreign word to many Christians in terms of their lifestyles, in terms of the Christian walk, and in terms of the Christian value system – Agape!

I think the best way to describe what this word "Agape" means, as compared to "Phileo" is to first tell you that they are miles apart in their meanings. In fact, in many ways, these two words are almost opposites. "Phileo Love" is a <u>PREFERENTIAL</u>, kind of love, it's what I like!

Agape love is a <u>SACRIFICIAL</u> and <u>BENEVOLENT</u> kind of love or <u>BENEVOLENT AFFECTION</u> . The emphasis for Agape love is on <u>others</u>. It is what I am willing to do for others. It's like a sacrificial kind of love that we parents generally have for our children.

- I DON'T CARE WHAT OUR KIDS HAVE DONE, THEY MAY BE <u>DOPING</u>, <u>DEALING</u>, <u>KILLING</u> OR <u>STEALING</u>, BUT THEY ARE STILL OUR CHILDREN, AND WE LOVE THEM. WE WILL DO WHAT WE CAN FOR THEM. I KNOW...I BEEN THERE! MANY OF US HAVE HORROR STORIES ABOUT OUR CHILDREN, BUT THEY ARE OURS.

- WE DON'T CARE WHETHER THAT LOVE IS RECIPROCATED, OR GIVEN BACK OR NOT. THEY

ARE STILL OUR CHILDREN AND WE LOVE THEM, AND WILL DO FOR THEM, EVEN THOUGH WE MIGHT BE DISAPPOINTED, MAD OR ANGRY AT THEM, OR THEIR ACTIONS.

• OH I CAN STILL HEAR MY MOTHER TELLING ME "BOY" I BROUGHT YOU HERE AND IF YOU DON'T ACT RIGHT I WILL TAKE YOU AWAY FROM HERE! BUT SHE LOVED ME!

Does that sound familiar to you? Let's pause for a moment and consider the perfect illustration of this "Agape" type love. Turn to a familiar scripture, John 3:16. We read at the beginning:

"For God so AGAPE the world, that He gave his only begotten Son, that whosoever believeth in Him should not perish, but have everlasting life."
[John 3:16]

Yes, Agape love is a "God like" love! You see God loved us so much until he was willing to <u>SACRIFICE</u> his most precious possession, his son, and allow him to come to earth as a man and hang, bleed and die on Calvary's Cross, that we might be free from the "WAGES OF SIN" (which is death) and have access to "salvation", which is a "<u>DELIVERANCE</u>" from the wages of our transgressions. That single act of Christ dying on the cross sacrificing his life for you and me, is the personification of what love really is. And that act (dying for us) is also the perfect picture of one of God's attributes, love. 1 John 4:16 teaches us that "God is Love". That is "AGAPE LOVE".

So, what does that mean for those of us who are followers of Christ? We say that we are the "sons and daughters of the Mot High God', we love to say "I'm a child of God". If we then are who we say we are, then the Godly attribute of love, "agape", should be manifested in us at all times. And that is the standard of love that God commands us to abide by. You see, it is impossible to exhaust God's love for us. And if we are like him, as his children, it is impossible to exhaust our love for others because our love flows from the spirit of God within us. That is why scriptures such as Matthew 5:44 which tells us to love our enemies, are problematical for many of us. This Agape love is typified by Jesus' death on the Cross!

- THIS IS NOT SOME TYPE OF "ETHNO-CENTRIC," OR "SELF-CENTERED" KIND OF LOVE.

- THIS "AGAPE" LOVE IS NOT A WEAK, "WISHY-WASHY," INCONSISTENT KIND OF LOVE. I CAN'T LOVE MY ENEMIES TODAY AND HATE THEM TOMORROW

- THIS "AGAPE" LOVE CANNOT BE DESCRIBED AS A WELL MEANING, "PASSIVE THOUGHT"... THAT TRANSLATES INTO A "NON-RESPONSIVE" INACTION. GOD "DID" SOMETHING ABOUT OUR PLIGHT!!

"AGAPE" love focuses on how we can meet the needs of others, and not ourselves. It changes us from having a selfish "how I feel" attitude, to a "how can I help them" attitude. It is an AGGRESSIVE and ACTION form of love that we are all capable of GIVING because e first received it. When God deposited the attribute of love in us, he gave us the RIGHT, and the POWER and the COMMANDMENT to give it to others!

The writer of Hebrews says that we can do that because our evil conscience has been sprinkled by the blood of Jesus which cleanses us. Paul told young Timothy in 1st Timothy 5 that this love sprang, or comes forth from:

- A PURE HEART:

- A GOOD CONSCIENCE: AND

- A SINCERE FAITH:

I said at the beginning of this sermon that we need to revisit this idea of Godly love from time to time.

- WE NEED TO DO A SELF-EVALUATION TO SEE HOW WE STACK UP WITH GOD'S EXPECTATION OF HIS CHILDREN. PAUL TELLS US IN 2 CORINTHIANS 13:5 THAT WE NEED TO "EXAMINE OURSELVES"

- WE NEED TO SEE IF WE ARE BEING OBEDIENT TO GOD'S WORD IN REPLICATING THIS CRITICAL ATTRIBUTE OF LOVE, IN FACT

- WE NEED TO SEE IF WE ARE NOT ONLY "TALKING THE TALK," BUT ALSO "WALKING THE WALK."

In Matthew, Chapter 22, when the Pharisees questioned Jesus about what was the greatest commandment of them all. He didn't list just one, but two. Both of them was about "agape" love. Let's look at Matthew 22:37-39:

"Jesus said to him, 'You shall AGAPE the Lord, your God with all your heart, with all your soul, and with all your mind.' This is the first and great commandment. And the second is like it: you shall AGAPE your neighbor as yourself.'"
[Matthew 22:37-39]

Think about it, I know that there were <u>many</u> times that God was not satisfied with me and my actions. But he did not stop loving me! He permitted me an opportunity to get things right. And, he keeps on loving me. That's the way our love should be, not giving up on others.

Some of us may think that loving some people are beyond us. But God placed in all of us his nature to love beyond our comprehension. But, we have to "energize" or "activate" that

Godly nature that we have in us. We as God's children must learn to love UNEQUIVOCABLY and UNCONDITIONALLY! We cannot be "phony lovers". Paul said in Romans 12:9 that our love should not be a "dissimulation" or hypocrisy. It must be genuine.

> *"Greater AGAPE has no one than this, than to lay down one's life for a friend." [John 15:13]*

The greatest manifestation of Godly love is to be ready to lay down one's life for a friend. Jesus dies on Calvary's Cross because he counted us as his friends, his family. Husbands ought to be willing to die for the sake of protecting their wives welfare, as Jesus died for us. And if Godly love is to be a "feeling", it should be a feeling of our sense of concern for those that we come in contact with. That feeling then becomes a prelude to our subsequent actions.

Thinking "good thoughts" and having "good feelings" about our neighbors sounds good. But it is simply not enough. We ought to be willing to "be there" to "stand in the gap" for those you don't even particularly care for. Isn't that an awesome, powerful kind of love?

In the English language there's a word called "synergism". It's a condition wherein the total impact of something is greater than the sum of the parts. That is the way Agape love is. The receivers receive more than you gave them. You receive more than you gave of yourself. "That" is the love that God wants us to demonstrate daily.

I want to close by reminding us of a few examples of what God's Word directs us to do. These examples are all based upon the "Agape" love that we Christians should exemplify in our daily walk with Christ.

"If thy enemy hungers, feed him. If he thirst, give him drink" [Romans 12:20]

"We then who are strong enough ought to bear the infirmities of the weak." [Romans 15:1]

"Bear ye one another's burdens." [Galatians 6:2]

Let us then, as Christians, become "doers" of God's Word instead of just "hearers". It is why we are here on this earth. It is "THE" purpose that God has ordained for ALL of his children

AMEN

JESUS: THE HUMAN-NESS OF THE DIVINE

"And the Word was made flesh, and dwell among us, and we beheld His glory, the glory as of the only begotten Son of the Father, Full of grace and truth."
[John 1:14]

During each Christmas season, many, if not most, Christians celebrate December 25th as the day in which we celebrate the birth of our Lord and Savior, Jesus Christ. This is not the exact day that Jesus was born, but is the day that many Christians have chosen to "commemorate" his birth.

What I wish to do in this sermon is to talk briefly about the nature of his coming and how God told his chosen people, and even told them where Jesus would be born. So, let me begin by considering a few ancient Biblical prophecies that told God's people about the coming of Jesus Christ. This is because:

- *IF* JEHOVAH GOD IS A GOD THAT DOES NOT CHANGE, AS HE DESCRIBES HIMSELF AT MALACHI 3:6, AND

- *IF* GOD SENT HIS WORD THROUGH HIS PROPHETS THAT HE WAS GOING TO DO A SPECIFIC THING, (IN THIS CASE, SEND FORTH HIS SON), AND

- *IF* WHAT GOD SAID CAME TO PASS, (AND I KNOW THAT IT DID)

- *THEN* WHAT DOES THAT TELL YOU AND ME ABOUT JEHOVAH GOD'S FAITHFULNESS TO HIS WORD?

For that reason I would like to look at two of God's prophecies, that God shared with the Prophet Isaiah and the Prophet Micah in

213

the Old Testament. I also must note that both of these prophecies were spoken approximately 700 years before Jesus Christ was born! First the Prophet Isaiah talked about Jehovah God's Son's conception at Isaiah 7:14:

> *"Therefore the Lord Himself shall give you a sign;*
> *Behold a virgin shall conceive, and bear a Son, and*
> *shall call His name Immanuel." [Isaiah 7:14]*

Next, we look at the prophecy from one of Isaiah's contemporaries, the Prophet Micah. The Lord told him where God's Son was going to be born:

> *"But thou, Bethlehem, Ephratah, though thou be*
> *little among all the thousands of Judah, yet out of thee*
> *shall come forth unto Me that is to be ruler in Israel;*
> *whose goings forth have been from of old, from*
> *everlasting." [Micah 5:2]*

Think about the awesome nature of these prophecies. We know now that both of these prophecies were fulfilled, even though the fulfillment occurred approximately seven hundred years later.

This person, this man, this Son of God that we call Jesus Christ, was in so many ways just like you and me:

- HE WALKED UPON THE FACE OF THIS EARTH, JUST LIKE YOU AND ME

- HE HAD FEELINGS AND EMOTIONS, JUST LIKE YOU AND ME

- HE WAS A MAN THAT EXPERIENCED SADNESS, AND SORROW, AND SHED TEARS AND HIS BLOOD, JUST LIKE YOU AND ME!

What a man Jesus was. But yet he was also the Son of God! He came to earth to redeem us by paying for our sins. Even though he sat at the right hand of his Father, Jehovah God, in the heavenly realm, he was willing to give up his throne and come down to earth to die that DISPICABLE and HORRENDOUS death at that Cross at Calvary. He did that so that, in spite of all of our sins, that if we chose, we could be his family! What a love story.

> *"For God so loved the world, that He gave His only begotten Son, that whosoever believeth in Him should not perish, but have everlasting life." [John 3:16]*

Doesn't that sound like some kind of a fairytale? It did to me when I first heard it. Yet, that is why we celebrate the birth of Jesus Christ, our Lord and Savior. I like to call him, because of his human-ness, the Humanity of the Divine!!

Most of us know the story of Jesus' birth, but the Word of God gives us more evidence that Jesus, in spite of being the Son of Jehovah God, Jesus was born here on earth as a human child. And as such, he grew up like you and me. In fact, he had to grow into maturity before he could go about the mission that his father had sent him here for. Let me just share a couple of scriptures from the 2nd chapter of Luke concerning the child Jesus:

> *"And the child grew, and waxed strong in the spirit, filled with wisdom: and the grace of God was upon Him." [Luke 2:40]*

> *"And Jesus increased in wisdom and stature, and in favor with God and man." [Luke 2:52]*

When Jesus began his ministry here on earth, because he was God incarnate, he found it necessary to remind people of his human-ness by continually referring to himself, not as the Son of God, but as the Son of Man! You can find examples of this at Matthew 9:6, Mark 14:21; 14:62, Luke 7:34 and 22:69.

215

There is so much that can be said about Jesus because of his presence here on this earth as a man, which makes it very difficult for many people to accept him as the Son of God. However, they would be willing to accept my off springs as "Swifts". They even concede that Jesus' reported accomplishments, which are well documented, as a result of some kind of supernatural power, he simply could not have been what he professed to be, Jesus the "Messiah", or "Christ". And many concluded that if he was the "son of Man' then he had to be a sinner, just like them. Even though God's Word on this matter is very clear!

> *"For God made Christ, who never sinned, to be the offering for our sin, so that we could be made right with God through Christ." [2nd Corinthians 5:21]*

As I close, you can imagine how the Pharisees, the Jewish Priests, the Scribes and the Sadducees felt when Jesus made statements such as:

> *"Let not your heart be troubled: ye believe in God, believe also in Me. (2) In My Father's house are many mansions: if it were not so, I would have told you. I go to prepare a place for you, (3) And if I go and prepare a place for you, I will come again, and receive you unto Myself; that where I am, there ye may be also."*
> *[John 14:1-3]*

Or a statement like this:

> *"Jesus said unto him, I am the way, the truth, and the life: no man cometh unto the Father, but by me."*
> *[John 14:6]*

Many back then just could not accept the fact that Jesus, the "Human" man, was in fact the Son of God! It is still that way today. Many people who call themselves Christians will "say"

216

they believe that Jesus is their Lord and Savior, but continue to walk in a manner that reveals otherwise.

If we love Jesus Christ, the only begotten Son of Jehovah God, all of us need to demonstrate that love in accordance with Jesus' command at John 10:10 that we obey his commandments.

AMEN

MY GOD IS ABLE!

*"Now to Him who is able to do exceedingly
abundantly above all that we ask or think, according to
the power that works in us," [Ephesians 3:20]*

One day I was asked to speak to a group of young people who had been incarcerated. And I also knew that many of them had never been exposed to the Word of God. I felt that this was a very important assignment, and I wanted to introduce them to the Word of God in a way that at least some of them, or even one of them, would have some "food for thought".

As I was contemplating what I was going to speak on, I began thinking about Ephesians 3:20. I sometimes use that scripture as a benediction, so it is a very familiar scripture to me. I went and got my Bible and started reading it again, and the Holy Spirit began to uncover some of the relevancy of that scripture in our day to day lives. And I must admit, I had not thought about that scripture in that context. That is why I am mindful of the fact that the Word of God is inexhaustible! I don't care how many times that you read it, it continues to reveal to us more and more knowledge!

Now I can't talk to you as I talked with those young people, because they needed to hear the very basic principles of God's doctrines. Otherwise, I had/have to feed them the "milk" of God's Word. You are more advanced than that, so I need to step up a notch in this sermon so that you can enjoy the Word that I shared with those young folk.

Let us begin by going back and looking at Ephesians 3:20. Again, the Apostle Paul describes God as one who was able (listen to this) to do <u>EXCEEDINGLY</u> and <u>ABUNDANTLY</u> above <u>ALL</u> that we can <u>ASK</u> of him, and more that you and I can even <u>THINK OF</u>! Now that is an awesome statement. And yet, every day many of us that call ourselves Christians act like we don't believe that. We "act" like God is not able or his Word does not apply to us! You see:

- WHAT THAT MEANS IS THAT GOD CAN DO MORE THAN WE CAN EVEN THINK OF IN OUR FINANCIAL SITUATIONS. PAUL SAID THAT WE NEED TO ASK GOD FOR WHAT WE WANT.

- IT MEANS THAT GOD CAN DO MORE THAT WE CAN IMAGINE IN OUR HEALTH SITUATIONS. .PAUL SAYS THAT WE NEED TO ASK.

- IT MEANS THAT YOU CAN CALL ON GOD TO IMPROVE AND HEAL ALL OF OUR RELATIONSHIPS IN OUR FAMILIES, IN OUR COMMUNITIES, AND ALL OVER THE WORLD! ALL WE NEED TO DO IS ASK!

- AND....AS A FINAL EXAMPLE....GOD CAN HEAL AND PROTECT OUR OFF-SPRINGS, AND I KNOW THAT WE ALL DESIRE THAT! IS THAT WHAT PAUL SAID IN THAT VERSE?? "ALL" THAT WE ASK? SO, WE NEED TO ASK!

Now let me ask a few questions for "my" comments and "your" consideration.

1.   WHY IS GOD WILLING TO BE SO GRACIOUS AND LOVING TO US?

I want to begin by reminding us as to why God made us. And that is the fact that God made man to be a great deal like him. God wanted to have a family. Can you believe that? He had already created himself a son to be like him. He had already created the angels to be his servants. He had already created the animals of the land, the fish of the sea and the birds of the air, but God wanted something else, he wanted a family! So he decided to make man. Let's go back again and take a look at God's creation of man. Turn your bibles to Genesis 1:26:

> *"Then God said let us make man in Our image, according to Our likeness; let them have dominion over the fish of the sea, over the birds of the air, and over the cattle, over all the earth and over every creeping thing that creeps on the earth." [Genesis 1:26] NKJV*

You see the words, "have dominion", what do think that means? Yes, God created this special creation called <u>Man</u> to be members of his family, and to have dominion. That is to be God's over his creation, the earth. I want you to think about how awesome that reality is. I want you to understand who you are! I want us to come away with a clear feeling about why God created us different from any other of his creations. Don't feel bad if you don't understand. King David, the Psalmist, had the same problem. One day as King David was sitting around thinking about life and creation in general, he began to commune with Jehovah God, his Father. His thoughts were later in the 8th number of the Psalms. Here he said, beginning at verse 3:

> *"When I consider Your heavens the work of Your fingers, The moon and the stars, which You have ordained, What is man that You are mindful of him, and the son of man that You visit him? For You have made him a little lower than the angels, and You have crowned him with glory and honor, You have made him to have dominion over the works of your hands: You have put all things under his feet..*
> *(Psalm 8:3-6) NKJV*

We are made different from any of God's other creations. We ought to shout for joy when we come to the realization of who we are because God created us specially. First is to have dominion her on earth, and later to be members of his heavenly family.

Think about this. He didn't make any of the beasts or animals of the land to be his family.

- NOT EVEN THE LION....WHO WE CALL THE KING OF THE FORESTS
- THEY CAN NEVER BE COUNTED AS SONS & DAUGHTERS OF THE MOST HIGH GOD! BUT YOU AND I CAN.
- NOT EVEN THE WHALES OF THE SEAS
- NOT EVEN THE EAGLES OF THE AIR

God created them for other purposes, but not to be members of his family. But you and I were created for a special purpose! God placed many of his attributes in us so that we could think, we could love, and so that we could forgive. Animals and birds can't do that. One other point that I would like to make at this time is, if we claim to be Christians, we certainly can't claim to be ourselves. Nonetheless, many of us try to act like we are our own Gods.

You know, I was thinking about this issue one day when I thought, I don't know a single human being that lives here on earth that can create or construct a living man, with all of these billions of cells that we are made of. But I hear King David the Psalmist again talking with God and I heard him say in the 139th Psalm:

"For You formed my inward parts; You covered me while I was in my mother's womb- I will praise You, for I am fearfully and wonderfully made:..."

You see, David was talking to his <u>CREATOR</u> and that's who "we" belong to! In my case I just couldn't "get it". Therefore, I could not get my walk right with Christ until I was able to internalize those two bits of knowledge about why God created me and what he had stored up for me. Not only in heaven, but right here on earth also.

Now I know that it appears that I have lost sight of my subject, that God is able. But that is exactly what this sermon is all about. I want you to understand that what Paul is saying is "truth beyond a shadow of a doubt". But I don't want us to conclude that all we have to do is just sit back and wait on god. There are some things that God requires that you and I have to do in order for God to respond to our needs with all of this power that he has, and his desire to rain his power of love down upon us. So maybe if I don't answer another question, I need to answer this one:

2. WHAT DO WE HAVE TO DO TO "ACTUALIZE" GOD'S POWER IN OUR LIVES?

There is an important clue in Paul's letter to the Ephesians that we used as a foundation for this sermon. Let's turn our Bible back to Ephesians 3:20:

> *"Now unto Him that is able to do exceedingly abundantly above all that we ASK or think, according to the power that works in us." {Ephesians 3:20}*

I want to key on that phrase "all that we ask or think". The first thing that I want to say to you is – here on earth you and I just can't go to anybody and ask for anything, and expect it to be given, unless we have a right standing with that person or organization to do so. Otherwise, there is normally some kind of criteria that the recipient must meet. I want you to remember that because it is critical. Let me give you a few examples:

- BILL & MELINDA GATES ARE BILLIONAIRES AND ARE VERY LIBERAL ABOUT GIVING THEIR MONEY

222

AWAY. IN FACT, THEY CAN'T GIVE IT AWAY FAST
ENOUGH! YOU THINK I CAN JUST GET UP AND
CONTACT THEM AND ASK FOR A MEASLEY
MILLION DOLLARS & GET IT.? OF COURSE NOT!!

- WELL, WHAT ABOUT WARREN BUFFET. OR
MAYBE OPRAH WINFREY, BOTH OF WHOM ARE
BILLIONAIRES. MAYBE I COULD ASK ONE OF
THOSE FOR A HUNDRED THOUSAND FOR MY
CAUSE. YOU THINK THAT I WOULD GET IT?
PROBABLY NOT, UNLESS I MET THEIR CRITERIA,
OR GUIDELINES.

You see, all of these have it, and all of these are givers. But I
would venture to say that I would never get past the front doors
with that kind of request. You see, certain conditions must be met
if I am to expect my request to be honored.

Well my Christian friends, our God is also that way. Let me
summarize, before I share with you some scriptures, by simply
saying, we must be in the right relationship with God if we expect
him to answer our prayers, petitions or requests. And secondly,
we must ASK HIM! And we need to be careful about "how" we
ask him. After all, if God is your Father, then we ask him
believing that he is going to give it to us. I like the way the writer
of Hebrews says it in Hebrews 4:16:

> *"Let us therefore come BOLDLY to the throne of
> grace, That we may obtain mercy and find grace to help
> in time of need." {Hebrews 4:16}*

Now let's look at a few scriptures. First let's go back and see
what God told his chosen people, the Israelites, through Moses.
Turn your Bibles to Deuteronomy the 28th chapter. I want to read
the 1st and 2nd verses:

"Now it shall come to pass, if you diligently obey the voice of the Lord your God, to observe carefully all His commandments which I command you today, that the Lord your God will set you high above all nations on the earth....And all these blessings shall come upon you and overtake you...BECAUSE YOU OBEY THE VOICE OF THE LORD YOUR GOD!!" {Deut. 28:1-2}

That is what God requires of those who are his. They must:

- OBEY HIS VOICE;

- OBSERVE HIS COMMANDMENTS

And then they will be rewarded because they obey the voice of God. And then King David says that you have to seek him. In Psalms 24 verse 4, King David says:

- *"I SOUGHT THE LORD AND HE HEARD ME, AND DELIVERED ME FROM ALL MY FEARS."*

I like the way James says it in James 4:8. He says draw near to God and God will draw near to you. I bet you, if you don't have a loving and obedient relationship with your earthly father, you may be wasting your time to ask for anything. Well God the Father is that way also. Let's quote one more scripture before we close. This one is about asking for what you want. Paul wrote in Philippians 4:6:

"Be anxious for nothing, but in everything by PRAYER and SUPPLICATION, with thanksgiving, let your request be made known to God." {Philippians 4:6}

Yes, God is able to answer any petition that his sons and daughters place before him. And he knows our needs and desires before we tell him. However, God has some expectations of his children, just like we have expectations of ours. And if we walk in harmony with the Word of God, obeying his commandments, we are entitled as his children to all of the promises and blessings that God has promised us in his Word. We don't have to be mealy mouthed, like we have no right to be there, when we come before God's presence with our petitions. On the contrary, the writer of Hebrews says that we ought to come boldly before his throne, like we got every right to be there as sons and daughter of the Most High God!

Yes, God is able to do exceedingly abundantly above all that we can ask or think. I believe that, I know that it is true and I want you also to have faith. In the Word of God, not only is he ABLE, but he is also FAITHFUL!

AMEN

Made in the USA
Columbia, SC
23 April 2018